crazy for chipotle

by Lynn Nusom

photography by
Christopher Marchetti

 northland publishing

My deep gratitude and thanks to my wife, Guylyn Morris Nusom,
for all her help with this book. She developed the concept
and was invaluable in helping with the research, recipe development,
and proofreading of the manuscript.

Text © 2004 by Lynn Nusom
Photographs © 2004 by Northland Publishing
All rights reserved.

This book may not be reproduced in whole or in part, by any means
(with the exception of short quotes for the purpose of review), without permission of the publisher.
For information, address Permissions, Northland Publishing, 2900 North Fort Valley Road, Flagstaff, Arizona 86001.

www.northlandpub.com

Composed in the United States of America
Printed in China

Edited by Tammy Gales, Designed by Katie Jennings
Production supervised by Donna Boyd
Photography by Christopher Marchetti

The TABASCO® marks, bottle, and label designs are registered trademarks and servicemarks exclusively of
McIlhenny Company, Avery Island, LA 70513. www.TABASCO.com

We would like to offer a special "thank you" to Lisa Aguiñaga-Mansfield
at De Colores del Barrio/Café Olé for letting us photograph her beautiful Mexican wares.

FIRST IMPRESSION 2004
ISBN 0-87358-861-4

Library of Congress Cataloging-in-Publication Data

Nusom, Lynn.
Crazy for chipotle / by Lynn Nusom.
p. cm.
Includes index.
1. Cookery (Hot peppers) 2. Cookery, American—Southwestern style.
I. Title.
TX803.P46N85 2004
541.6'384—dc22   2004041538

contents

This has been a fun book to write! The more I sampled, cooked, and tried southwestern recipes the more interested I became in different varieties of chile. When we moved back to my wife's hometown in southern New Mexico, just down the road from Hatch, NM—the chile capital of the World—I tried New Mexico red and green chiles, jalapeños, and numerous varieties grown in Mexico. After sampling so many great chile flavors, it was a natural progression to the wonderful, smoky, rich taste of chipotle.

Growing up in the Northeast, even though my family was in the food business, I was only familiar with two spicy dishes: chili, made with ground beef, canned tomatoes, kidney beans, and chili powder; and chilidogs, which were usually hotdogs topped with a similar concoction of hamburger, tomato, and chili powder. My wife, on the other hand, was born and raised in the Southwest, and she was fortunate enough to grow up on chile rellenos, green and red enchiladas, and steaming bowls of Red—considered real chili in the Southwest.

I soon learned that chile was spelled with an "e" when it referred to the fruit of the chile plant and with an "i" when it denoted a bowl of chili. Being a quick study, I also learned the differences between various New Mexico green chiles, and on trips around the Southwest, I experienced a myriad of ways of preparing chile dishes. But the traditional dishes I discovered during this time were pretty much relegated to the Southwest.

Approximately twenty years ago, the American public, tired of the same, old bland food, started experimenting with new and different dishes, including chile dishes. Food writers and television cooking shows picked up on chiles, and suddenly, chiles broke into the mainstream. Salsa replaced ketchup as the number one condiment in the U.S., and people from coast to coast started adding heat to meals with jalapeños, green chiles, dried red chile, and even habaneros. But even though jalapeños, which become chipotles when dried and smoked, skyrocketed as the most popular chile in the country, chipotles were left in obscurity.

In Mexico, however, the chipotle has a long and rich history. Historians think the chipotle dates back many centuries, and some researchers even speculate that the Aztecs perfected the smoking procedure so that the thick, fleshy, red jalapeños could be preserved. In the sixteenth century, when the Spanish explorers and priests arrived, it is reported that they ate dishes such as teatzin with chipotle. Today, chipotles are still used in Mexico in a wide variety of dishes, including meat in adobo sauce, grilled meat rubbed with chipotle, and chipotles pickled with sugar, garlic, and herbs.

Like many trends, it's hard to determine just when chipotle moved into the mainstream, but no matter how or when it arrived—it has arrived! Chipotle has found its way onto the menus of restaurants as diverse as upscale Manhattan eateries to inexpensive fast-food chains, and other kinds of businesses are quickly jumping on the chipotle bandwagon as well. The McIlhenny Company, producers of everyone's favorite hot sauce— TABASCO®, has added a Chipotle Pepper Sauce to their product line, and such venerable food purveyors as French's and McCormick's are also adding chipotle to their lines.

The reason for all of this popularity? It's simple! The smoking and drying process of converting jalapeños into chipotles results in a rich, smoky flavor that improves many dishes, including those we thought couldn't be improved. Chipotles provide a depth of flavor that few other chiles can offer.

Remember, as with most chiles, chipotles are HOT! Chipotles register 5,000 to 10,000 Scoville Units, which puts them at a 7 on the heat scale.

For comparison, jalapeños register a 5 on the heat scale, and habaneros register a 10 on the heat scale. Always remember to adjust the amount of chipotle in these recipes to suit your heat tolerance. If you, or your guests, don't have a high tolerance for heat, start with a very small amount of chipotle. If you are chile aficionados and believe "the hotter-the-better," then increase the amount to your liking.

To sum it up, we're *Crazy for Chipotle*—and captured in this beautiful book are some of our favorite chipotle recipes. We sincerely hope that you will enjoy them as much as we do.

¡viva La chipotle!

CHIPOTLE BASICS

THE CHIPOTLE HAS one of the most complex flavors in the world of chiles. The heat of the jalapeño coupled with the smoke-drying process produces a depth of flavor and aroma that is wholly unique. However, since chipotles come from a variety of ripe, red jalapeños, they are not necessarily created equal. The main variety of chipotle, the chile ahumado, which literally means "smoked chile," is rather stiff and is a grayish-tan color. Another popular variety, the morita, which means "little blackberry," is dark red and more pliable, because it's not smoked as long as the chile ahumado.

These and the numerous other varieties of chipotles available today translate into a wide variety of commercial products, including whole chipotles, chipotle powder, crushed chipotle, and chipotles canned in adobo sauce. Why not try them all and then choose the taste and look you prefer for each of your favorite dishes.

CHIPOTLE IN ADOBO SAUCE

The easiest and least expensive way to find chipotles are canned in adobo sauce. There are several manufacturers in Mexico shipping this product to the United States, and you can buy them in most supermarkets in the Southwest. However, if they are unavailable in your area, you can find them in markets specializing in Hispanic foods or on the Internet.

Many of the recipes in this book call for an entire 7-ounce can of chipotle in adobo sauce. However, when the recipe calls for less than the entire can of chipotles

or if you want less heat, use the desired amount and then place the remainder of the chipotles in a plastic zip-lock freezer bag and freeze for later use.

When using chipotles in adobo sauce, you may or may not want to rinse the adobo sauce off the chipotle. This depends on whether or not you want the tomato-vinegar taste in the dish you're making.

WHOLE, DRIED CHIPOTLES

You can also use whole dried chipotles in your recipes. To use whole chipotles, remove the stems, and then chop or grind the chipotles. They are especially good used this way when you want the flecks of chipotle to show in the finished dish.

Whole chipotles are not always easy to come by. Your best bet to find them is in Mexican food markets. However, be prepared—they are often more expensive than many other chiles, but you'll find the added flavor is well worth it. You can also buy whole chipotles in bulk over the Internet, so if you really love the taste, but can't find them locally, this is a great option.

CHIPOTLE POWDER

Chipotle powder, now made by several large manufacturers, is best used in dips, salad dressings, and some soups. Chipotle powders vary widely in the intensity of heat—many of them are not as strong as using the same amount of crushed whole chipotles or chipotle in adobo sauce. So, it's wise to cut, try, and taste before finishing off a dish.

3

CHIPOTLE SAUCE

Many companies, such as TABASCO®, have also caught on to the emerging popularity of chipotle and are making Chipotle Pepper Sauces. These are found in most supermarkets and are great in a wide variety of recipes. You can cook with it, or sprinkle a dash or two on any finished dish you want to give a kick. A little of this sauce on scrambled eggs, potatoes, or simple dishes such as macaroni and cheese will set your taste buds a tingle.

HOMEMADE CHIPOTLE

For those of you who are a little more daring and have a little more time on your hands, smoking your own chipotles might be the answer for you.

In Mexico, jalapeños are harvested when they have turned red and have partially dried on the plant. Large quantities are then placed on a metal or wooden rack in a large pit, which is connected by an underground tunnel to another pit where a fire is burning, and then they are smoked for days. Since this method is not very realistic at home, you can purchase red jalapeños at your local Farmer's Market or grocery store and then smoke them on a clean barbecue grill with a lid. (Make sure the grill is very clean, as the chipotles will soak up the previous flavors and result in bad-tasting chiles.)

The best wood for smoking chipotles is fruitwood or hardwoods such as oak, pecan, or mesquite. If you use mesquite, you will get chipotles that are tan in color like the tapico. Other types of wood will usually give you chipotles that more closely resemble the red moritas.

Light two small fires on each side of the grill, and place the jalapeños on the clean rack in the center, making sure that they are not directly over the flame. Close the lid and allow the chiles to absorb the smoke, making sure to rotate the chiles periodically so that they dry out evenly. When the chipotles are done, they should be stiff, light, and brownish in color. This process can take up to two days, but it will be well worth the effort.

At this point, you can use the whole chipotles immediately, preserve them in an air-tight container for later use, or decide to take them a step further and create chipotle in adobo sauce or chipotle powder. In order to make chipotle powder, you need to use a food dehydrator or an oven to take the last bit of moisture out of them. You can use an electric oven, gas oven, or electric dehydrator. First, make sure your room is well ventilated. Second, stretch cheesecloth across one of your oven racks and fasten it with ovenproof clips. Third, set the oven temperature to low, but not below 150° F. If you dry the chiles in an electric oven, prop the door open about 1 inch to allow the moisture from the chiles to vent. If you are using a gas oven, you can keep the door closed. Finally, let the chiles dry in the oven until they are light, stiff, and easy to break. Your homemade chipotle products will keep for years if kept cool and dry.

So, whether you're a novice just embarking on the exciting world of chiles or a seasoned veteran, I hope these hints and tips will help you enjoy the recipes in this book. No matter which form of chipotle you use, I know you'll be as crazy for chipotle as I am.

appetizers

These appetizers are the perfect way to introduce family and friends to the wonderful delights of chipotle. Serve one or two of these dishes with drinks or add a couple of them to a buffet table, and you'll give a marvelous lift to any festive gathering.

PINTO BEAN CHIPOTLE DIP

SMOKY CHILE CON QUESO

WARM BLACK BEAN DIP

PECAN CHEESE BALL

FIERY DEVILED EGGS

SHRIMP QUESADILLAS

BLUE CHEESE CHIPOTLE SPREAD

CRANBERRY-CHIPOTLE SPREAD

ARTICHOKE AND CHIPOTLE BRUSCHETTA

GARBANZO BEAN SPREAD

pinto bean chipotle dip

PINTO BEANS ARE TO SOUTHWESTERNERS what potatoes are to Midwesterners—they can be served at almost every meal. Served mashed or refried with eggs for breakfast, or on the side for lunch or dinner, pinto beans are the perfect accompaniment to a wide variety of dishes. With the addition of fiery chipotle in adobo sauce, they also make a splendid, crowd-pleasing dip.

Pick over the beans and discard any stones or bad beans. Place the beans in a large soup pot. Cover the beans with very hot water and let sit for an hour. Discard any floaters. Drain and rinse the beans under running water. Place the beans back in the pot, cover with water, and bring to a boil over high heat. Reduce the heat to low and simmer, covered, for 1 ½ to 2 hours or until the beans are tender, and then drain.

Heat the oil in a large skillet (cast iron works best) and sauté the onion for 3 to 4 minutes. Stir in the beans and mash with a potato masher. Cook on low heat until the beans are heated through, about 3 to 5 minutes. Stir the chipotle, garlic, cilantro, salt, and pepper into the beans. If necessary, add a little more olive oil to reach the desired consistency.

Serve at room temperature with tortilla chips or fresh slices of jicama, celery, red and green bell pepper, and cauliflower florets.

Makes 4 to 6 Servings

1 pound dried pinto beans
2 tablespoons extra virgin olive oil
1 medium yellow onion, coarsely chopped
1 (4-ounce) can chipotles in adobo sauce
2 cloves garlic, finely chopped
½ cup cilantro, chopped
1 teaspoon salt
½ teaspoon freshly ground black pepper

smoky chile con queso

I KNOW SOMEBODY out there is going to turn up their nose at using Velveeta. But, we know from long experience that Velveeta makes the best queso. It is so good, that your guests will be queuing up for this rich, smoky cheese dip at your next party. You can spoon this dip into a slow cooker, plug it in, and it will keep on a buffet table for a couple of hours. Although most Southwesterners serve it with tortilla chips, I also like to serve it with flavored wheat chips or even potato chips.

Combine all of the ingredients in a heavy-bottomed saucepan. Cook over low heat, stirring occasionally, until the cheese has melted and is warmed through, about 8 to 10 minutes. Spoon the mixture into a bowl or a warm slow cooker and let your imagination run riot picking out what to dip into it.
Makes 8 to 10 Servings

1 pound Velveeta, coarsely chopped into cubes
1/2 can evaporated milk
1/2 red bell pepper, seeded and finely diced
1/2 green bell pepper, seeded and finely diced
1 teaspoon garlic powder
1/2 teaspoon chipotle flakes
1/4 teaspoon TABASCO® brand Chipotle Pepper Sauce

warm black bean dip

BEAN DIPS, once relegated to family snacking, have now gone up-scale. Black beans, a staple of Caribbean and Latin American cooking, are now part of the southwestern cook's arsenal. Not only do they have a wonderful, unique, earthy taste, but the experts also say that beans are good for you.

Heat the oil in a skillet and sauté the onions over medium heat until soft. Stir in the black beans and mash with a potato masher. Then add the chicken broth, wine, cilantro, garlic, and chipotle and simmer until heated through, about 3 to 5 minutes. Stir in the lime juice.

Place the bean mixture in a shallow bowl and sprinkle the cheese over the top. Serve warm with white or blue corn tortilla chips.

Makes 4 to 6 Servings

2 tablespoons extra virgin olive oil
1 small yellow onion, finely chopped
2 (15-ounce) cans black beans, drained and rinsed
1 tablespoon chicken broth
1 tablespoon white wine
1 tablespoon fresh cilantro, finely chopped
1 clove garlic, squeezed through a garlic press
1 chipotle in adobo sauce, minced
Juice of 1 lime
1/2 cup Monterey Jack cheese, shredded

pecaN cheese BaLL

YES, I KNOW — you can pick up a cheese ball in the fancy cheese section of most supermarkets, especially around the holidays. And yes, I know — cheese balls are old fashioned. However, they are a great comfort food, and they are so good and so much better when you make them at home. They are perfect to serve at a cocktail buffet or to give as a hostess gift.

Place the coarsely chopped pecans in a food processor and pulse until crushed but not ground. Pour them into a shallow bowl and reserve. Place the Colby cheese, cream cheese, chipotle, horseradish, and parsley in a food processor. Process until well blended (if it is too stiff, add a few drops of extra virgin olive oil and process again).

Form the cheese mixture into a ball. If too soft, place it in the refrigerator for about 30 minutes or until firm. Roll the ball in the crushed pecan bits. Chill until ready to serve. Place on a plate and serve with good crackers or French bread. *Makes 8 to 10 Servings*

1 cup pecans, coarsely chopped
1 cup Colby cheese, grated
1 (8-ounce) package cream cheese
1 chipotle in adobo sauce, minced
1 teaspoon horseradish
1 teaspoon dried parsley

fiery deviled eggs

HOLIDAY DINNERS AT OUR HOUSE are not complete without deviled eggs. However, tired of the same, old eggs, we started experimenting with all sorts of additions to the egg yolk mixture, including green chile, chutney, curry powder, and turmeric. All these ingredients were good, but we found that chipotle is the best.

This particular variation takes this once mundane holiday dish to new heights. By the way, you don't have to wait for a holiday—these little deviled eggs are also extremely good with cocktails any day of the year.

Carefully remove the yolks from the whites of the hard boiled eggs. Place the yolks in a bowl and mash them with a fork. Add the mayonnaise, sour cream, garlic salt, celery salt, black pepper, and chipotle. Mix well, and then spoon the mixture back into the egg white halves. Garnish the top of each half with an olive ring.
Makes 8 Servings

8 eggs, hard boiled, shelled, and cut in half lengthwise
1 tablespoon mayonnaise
1 tablespoon sour cream
$\frac{1}{4}$ teaspoon garlic salt
$\frac{1}{4}$ teaspoon celery salt
$\frac{1}{4}$ teaspoon freshly ground black pepper
1 chipotle in adobo sauce, puréed
4-5 black olives, sliced into rings

shrimp quesadillas

THE DAYS WHEN QUESADILLAS were no more than chopped green chiles and melted cheese in flour tortillas are a thing of the past. Quesadillas have jumped into the mainstream and can be made with anything that tickles your fancy. We particularly like seafood quesadillas for a light, not-too-filling appetizer. Serve this snack with a nice dry white wine or a light Mexican beer.

Preheat oven to 350° F. Mix the cheeses, green onions, chipotle, and cilantro in a medium bowl and set aside. Lightly brush one side of 4 of the tortillas with the olive oil and place the oiled side down on a baking sheet (with 8-inch tortillas, you might need to use 2 baking sheets). Top the tortillas with one half of the cheese mixture and equal portions of shrimp and mango. Sprinkle the remaining cheese evenly over the shrimp and mango. Top with the remaining tortillas and brush the top of the tortillas with olive oil. Bake for 8 to 10 minutes or until the cheese has melted.

Cut each quesadilla into quarters and serve with Fireworks Salsa (page 91), or for those looking for a salsa with more heat, serve with 1 (7-ounce) can of chipotles in adobo sauce, puréed.
Makes 4 to 6 Servings

1 cup Monterey Jack cheese, shredded
½ cup Cheddar cheese, shredded
2 green onions, with the white part and some of the green part, chopped
1 chipotle, stem removed and crushed
1 tablespoon fresh cilantro, chopped, or 1 teaspoon dried cilantro, crushed
8 (8-inch) flour tortillas
2 tablespoons extra virgin olive oil
1 pound large shrimp, cooked, peeled, deveined, and cut in half lengthwise
1 medium mango, coarsely chopped

bLue cheese chipotLe spread

ALTHOUGH PRACTICALLY EVERY SERVER in every restaurant rattles off blue cheese dressing as one of the choices with your salad order, there are many other ways to use this delectable cheese. Pickled chile and blue cheese are a remarkable pairing, and combining blue cheese with chipotle will delight the guests at your next party.

Put the blue cheese, bell pepper, sour cream, sun-dried tomatoes, and chipotle flakes in a food processor and process until smooth. Spoon the mixture into a serving bowl, cover, and place in the refrigerator for 1 hour or until firm.

When ready to serve, top with the green onions and crumbled bacon. Serve with slices of warm, crusty French bread. *Makes 6 to 8 Servings*

1 pound blue cheese, crumbled
1 red bell pepper, seeded and chopped
3 tablespoons sour cream
1 tablespoon sun-dried tomatoes, packed in oil
$1/2$ teaspoon chipotle flakes
2 green onions, with some of the green part, sliced
2 tablespoons crisp bacon crumbles

CRANBERRY-CHIPOTLE SPREAD

WE ENTERTAIN QUITE A BIT, and some of the favorite dishes in our repertoire use cream cheese as the base for wonderful spreads to put on crackers, pan tostados, or baguettes. This particular one is a favorite around the holidays, especially when fresh cranberries are easy to find.

Put the cranberries, orange peel, and nuts in a food processor and pulse rapidly four or five times until coarsely chopped. Add the chipotle, cilantro, and cream cheese and blend until smooth.

Spoon into a bowl, cover with plastic wrap, and refrigerate until ready to serve. Serve with good crackers, French bread, or Mexican pan tostados.
Makes 4 to 5 Servings

1 cup fresh cranberries

2 teaspoons orange peel, freshly grated

$^1\!/_2$ cup pecans or walnuts, coarsely chopped

1 chipotle in adobo sauce, coarsely chopped

1 tablespoon fresh cilantro, finely chopped

1 (8-ounce) package cream cheese (you can use the low fat variety)

artichoke and chipotle bruschetta

THE FRESH, CLEAN TASTE of artichoke underscored by garlic, cilantro, and the fiery bite of chipotle makes this bruschetta perfect as an appetizer with a glass of red wine or as a starter for a dish of linguine with clam sauce.

Preheat oven to 400° F. Place the artichoke hearts, garlic, parsley, chipotle, salt, and lime juice in a food processor and coarsely chop. Add the oil and process until it becomes a spreadable mixture but not smooth.

Slice the bread diagonally into thick slices. Spread the artichoke mixture on one side of each slice of bread. Place the bread, uncoated side down, on an ungreased baking sheet and bake for approximately 8 to 10 minutes or until the bread is lightly toasted. *Makes 6 to 8 Servings*

1   cup artichoke hearts, drained
2   cloves garlic
1   tablespoon fresh parsley, chopped, or 1 teaspoon dried parsley
1   chipotle in adobo sauce
$1/4$ teaspoon salt
Juice of 1 lime
$1/4$ cup extra virgin olive oil
1   large loaf Italian bread

Garbanzo Bean Spread

THIS RECIPE IS A VARIATION of the traditional Middle-Eastern dish called hummus. This version is very rich and has a wonderful smoky zip! This spread is good to take to a potluck or a picnic, because it will keep for a couple of hours without being refrigerated. We like to serve it with a variety of things such as corn chips, flour tortillas, pita bread, and crudités.

Place all of the ingredients, except the olive oil, in a food processor and blend. While processing the mixture, slowly drizzle the olive oil through the feeder tube and continue to blend until smooth.

Spoon the dip into a pretty glass bowl and surround it with an assortment of good crackers, pita bread, or fresh veggies. *Makes 4 to 6 Servings*

1   clove garlic, cut in half
$^1/_2$ teaspoon salt
1   (15-ounce) can garbanzo beans, drained
1   tablespoon fresh parsley, chopped
Juice of 1 lemon
$^1/_2$ teaspoon chipotle powder
$^1/_2$ cup extra virgin olive oil

saLads

The salads in this book feature a wide range of ingredients and appease a variety of tastes. We're all used to the ubiquitous small dinner salad served before restaurant meals; however, salads can be much more than that. The spectacularly rich flavor of chipotle used in the following recipes adds a new dimension to the average salad.

spicy grilled corn salad

FOR A BREAK FROM THE TRADITIONAL green salad, try this delicious grilled corn salad. It blends the warmth of cumin and chipotle chiles with the crisp, cool textures of corn, zucchini, and red bell pepper. Serve this tasty dish on your next night of al fresco dining.

Husk the corn, remove the silk, and grill until the corn is tender and some of the kernels turn brown but are not blackened. Let cool. Using a sharp knife, cut the kernels off the ears and set aside.

In a separate large bowl, combine the olive oil, vinegar, cumin, chipotle powder, and garlic powder. Mix well and then stir in the corn, green onions, zucchini, black beans, and bell pepper. Toss to coat the vegetables with the dressing. Cover with plastic wrap and chill in the refrigerator for at least 1 hour. Toss again before serving.   *Makes 6 Servings*

2   ears fresh corn
2   tablespoons olive oil
2   tablespoons white wine vinegar
$\frac{1}{2}$ teaspoon ground cumin
$\frac{1}{4}$ teaspoon chipotle chile powder
$\frac{1}{4}$ teaspoon garlic powder
2   green onions, with all of the white portion and most of the green portion, sliced
1   zucchini, peeled and chopped
1   (15-ounce) can black beans, drained and rinsed
1   red bell pepper, seeded and chopped

garbanzo bean salad

GARBANZO BEANS WERE INTRODUCED to the New World by the Spanish. Since that time, the beans have been used throughout Mexico and are a favorite with many southwestern cooks. This dish, with its rustic, earthy flavor is simple, easy to prepare, and makes an outstanding light lunch when served with some sharp white Cheddar cheese and crusty sourdough bread.

To make the dressing, mix the olive oil, vinegar, lemon juice, garlic, and chipotle together in a small bowl. Set aside.

To make the salad, put the red onion, tomatoes, pimento or bell pepper, parsley, and garbanzo beans in a salad bowl. Pour the dressing over the vegetables and lightly toss.

Place 1 leaf of Romaine lettuce on individual plates, spoon the salad over the Romaine, and garnish with sprigs of parsley.   *Makes 4 to 6 Servings*

DRESSING:

- 2   tablespoons extra virgin olive oil
- 1   tablespoon rice vinegar
- 1   tablespoon fresh lemon juice
- 1   clove garlic, minced
- 1/2 teaspoon chipotle chile powder

SALAD:

- 1   large red onion, thinly sliced
- 2   large ripe tomatoes, coarsely chopped
- 1   pimento or red bell pepper, seeded and chopped
- 1   tablespoon fresh parsley, chopped
- 2   (15-ounce) cans garbanzo beans, drained and rinsed
- 4-6 large Romaine lettuce leaves
- Sprigs of parsley

pasta, broccoli, and black bean salad with chipotle ranch dressing

THIS RECIPE WAS ALMOST LEFT OUT of the book, which would have been a shame since it started the whole project. The idea for the book came about while my wife, Guylyn, and I were having lunch at a restaurant in Chandler, Arizona. There was a salad with chipotle ranch dressing on the menu, and, of course, we ordered it. As is our wont, we then tore it apart and knew we could make a better one. One thing led to another, and we thought that if chipotle was becoming so popular in eateries, then we needed to let others know about some of the chipotle recipes we'd been experimenting with over the years.

It's true—you can make your own ranch dressing. However, we came to the conclusion that you can't do better than adding chipotle in adobo sauce to a good bottled dressing.

To make the salad, cook the pasta according to package directions. Drain and rinse under cold running water. Let cool, and then place in the refrigerator for approximately 1 hour.

When the pasta is cool, add the broccoli, onion, black beans, and bell pepper. Lightly toss in a medium salad bowl. Garnish the salad with strips of cheese and sprigs of cilantro or parsley.

To make the dressing, purée the chipotles in a food processor, add the ranch dressing, and pulse until well mixed. Pour the dressing into a bowl and serve on the side so that your guests can spoon the desired amount onto their salad.

Makes 4 to 6 Servings

SALAD:

1 (12-ounce) package pasta, such as rotini
1 cup fresh broccoli florets, coarsely chopped
$\frac{1}{2}$ medium white onion, finely chopped
1 (15-ounce) can black beans, drained and rinsed
$\frac{1}{2}$ red bell pepper, seeded and diced
8-12 thin strips of white Cheddar cheese or baby Swiss cheese
Sprigs of cilantro or parsley

DRESSING:

$\frac{1}{2}$ (3 $\frac{1}{2}$-ounce) can chipotle in adobo sauce
1 (16-ounce) bottle prepared ranch dressing

Black bean and asparagus salad with chipotle dressing

REMEMBER THOSE AWFUL bean salads that used to show up at church suppers and Fourth of July picnics? Okay, so you liked them! This unlikely combination of black beans and asparagus is a real winner, especially when accented with tomatoes, green onions, capers, and some zany chipotle dressing.

To make the salad, place the beans, tomatoes, onions, and capers in a salad bowl. Sprinkle the lemon juice and olive oil over the vegetables and stir gently.

Place 2 lettuce leaves on each of 4 individual salad plates and spoon the salad onto the lettuce. Top each plate with 3 asparagus spears.

To make the dressing, put the red bell pepper, yogurt, chipotle, salt, and pepper in a food processor or blender and blend until smooth. Top the salad with the dressing and serve immediately.

Makes 4 Servings

SALAD:

2   (15-ounce) cans black beans, drained and rinsed
2   large ripe tomatoes, coarsely chopped
2   green onions, with some of the green portion, chopped
1   tablespoon capers, drained
1   tablespoon fresh lemon juice
1   tablespoon extra virgin olive oil
8   lettuce leaves
12 thin asparagus spears, steamed until just tender

DRESSING:

1   red bell pepper, roasted, peeled, and seeded
1   cup yogurt
1   chipotle chile in adobo sauce
$^1/_2$ teaspoon salt
$^1/_2$ teaspoon freshly ground black pepper

spinach salad with cucumber-chipotle dressing

SPINACH SALAD IS ONE OF THOSE DISHES that has, more or less, left the fine dining scene. When it was at the height of fashion, it was prepared with crisp, crumbled bacon. But suddenly, when everyone jumped on the low-fat bandwagon, this salad was no longer considered sensible eating. We still love raw spinach, so we devised a great dressing that eschews the bacon without losing the delicious flavor.

To make the dressing, place all of the dressing ingredients in a food processor and blend until smooth. Let stand at room temperature while you make the salad.

To make the salad, tear the spinach leaves into halves and put them in a salad bowl. Sprinkle the slices of onion and the prosciutto over the spinach. Pour the dressing over the salad and lightly toss. *Makes 4 to 6 Servings*

DRESSING:

- 1 cucumber, peeled and seeded
- 1/2 cup plain yogurt
- 1/2 cup mayonnaise
- 1 chipotle in adobo sauce
- 2 anchovies, packed in oil
- 1 teaspoon fresh ginger, grated
- 1/2 teaspoon celery salt
- 1 tablespoon Parmesan or Romano cheese, grated

SALAD:

- 1 (6-ounce) package fresh spinach leaves, well washed and dried
- 1 medium red onion, cut in half and thinly sliced
- 8 thin slices prosciutto, chopped

Lobster and avocado salad

LOBSTER IS ONE OF THOSE SPLURGE FOODS — it's expensive and not always easy to come by. But whenever I have a chance, I make a simple lobster salad that contains lobster, mayonnaise, and fresh parsley. My wife, however, is much more adventurous when it comes to lobster. She has experimented with all kinds of lobster dishes, and we love the rich smoky flavor of this salad for the bold statement it makes at an al fresco luncheon.

Place the chopped lobster and avocados in a glass bowl. In a separate small bowl, stir the chipotle powder and lime juice together. Pour over the lobster and avocados, cover with plastic wrap, place in the refrigerator, and let marinate for 30 minutes.

To make the dressing, combine all of the dressing ingredients in a small bowl and set aside.

Remove the lobster from the refrigerator and add the green onion and the chopped lettuce. Pour the dressing over the salad and lightly toss to coat well. Cover again and chill in the refrigerator for approximately 1 hour before serving.

Makes 4 Servings

SALAD:

2   lobster tails (approximately 1 ½ pounds total weight), cooked and coarsely chopped

2   avocados, peeled, seeded, and coarsely chopped

½ teaspoon chipotle powder

Juice of 2 limes

1   green onion, with some of the green portion, chopped

1   head of butter lettuce, coarsely chopped

DRESSING:

2   tablespoons extra virgin olive oil

1   tablespoon rice vinegar

1   clove garlic, minced

Salt, to taste

Freshly ground black pepper, to taste

CRAB COMPUESTA SALAD

KATY GRIGGS, the owner of La Posta restaurant in southern New Mexico, claims to have invented tostada compuestas in 1939 when she opened her eatery. My wife's mother and father were some of her first patrons. Her compuestas were deep fried corn tortillas that formed a cup filled with pinto beans, or refried beans, and cubes of pork in a red chile sauce.

Using the same technique for making the tortilla cups, we've found that filling them with an updated blend of crabmeat and vegetables, accented with the smoky richness of chipotle, makes a great lunch, especially when served with frosty margaritas.

Heat the oil in a heavy skillet over medium-high heat and fry the tortillas one at a time until they are not quite crisp. This will happen very fast, usually less than 1 minute. Scoop the tortillas out of the oil with a slotted spoon and place them, individually, over inverted coffee mugs. Let the tortillas cool on the mugs, and they will form crisp cups.

Place the crabmeat in a mixing bowl and add the celery, onions, peas, and cucumber. Mix well, and chill in the refrigerator for at least 1 hour.

To make the dressing, mix the dressing ingredients together in a small bowl, and then pour the dressing over the chilled crabmeat and vegetables. Mix lightly, and then spoon the mixture into the crisp tortilla cups. Top each filled cup with shredded lettuce and grated carrot. Garnish with 2 or 3 black olives and serve immediately.
Makes 4 Servings

SALAD:
1   cup vegetable oil
4   fresh (6-inch) corn tortillas
1   pound crabmeat, cooked, picked over, rinsed,
     and shredded
3   ribs celery, strings removed and finely chopped
3   green onions, chopped
1   cup small green peas, cooked, drained, and chilled
1   small cucumber, peeled, seeded, and coarsely chopped
1   cup lettuce, shredded
1/2 cup carrots, grated
8-12 black olives

DRESSING:
1   tablespoon fresh lime juice
1   tablespoon fresh orange juice
4   tablespoons plain yogurt
1   chipotle chile, stem removed and crushed
1   tablespoon fresh parsley, chopped

GRiLLeD pineappLe anD chicken saLaD with aDobo DRessing

THIS WARM SALAD with its vibrant colors and fiery chipotle dressing will put a touch of excitement into a summer garden party.

Many cooks find preparing fresh pineapple daunting. However, it is really easy once you get the knack. Wear lightweight gloves when peeling the pineapple to avoid getting pricked. Hold the pineapple upright by the spines and cut away the skin with a sharp knife. Cut straight down deep enough to get rid of the embedded pieces of skin and continue with straight downward cuts around the entire pineapple. Then cut off the top and bottom, and it becomes an easy job to core and slice the pineapple into rings.

To prepare the chicken, trim any excess fat and membranes from the chicken and rinse under cold water. Slice the chicken into strips ½-inch thick and place in a glass bowl.

In a separate bowl, mix together the extra virgin olive oil, lime juice, tequila, and garlic. Pour over the chicken and coat well. Cover with plastic wrap and chill for 1 to 2 hours. Remove from the refrigerator and bring to room temperature, approximately 10 to 15 minutes.

To make the dressing, place the chipotle, yogurt, and grapes in a food processor and blend until smooth. The dressing should be pale orange in color. Set aside.

To make and assemble the salad, arrange a leaf of purple kale and two leaves of Romaine on each of 4 large plates.

Heat a cast iron griddle on an open fire or stove burner. When hot, grill the chicken strips and pineapple rings until the chicken is done and the pineapple slices have browned on both sides. This will happen very quickly, about 3 to 5 minutes depending on how hot your fire is.

When the chicken and pineapple are done, place 2 rings of pineapple on each plate of lettuce leaves, and arrange the chicken strips over the pineapple. Spoon a tablespoon of the dressing over the top. Garnish each plate with half a green onion on each side and serve immediately. *Makes 4 Servings*

SALAD:

4 (4-ounce) boneless, skinless chicken breasts
2 tablespoons extra virgin olive oil
Juice of 1 lime
¼ cup gold tequila
1 clove garlic, squeezed through a garlic press
4 leaves of purple kale
8 leaves of Romaine
8 fresh pineapple rings, approximately ½-inch thick
4 green onions, including the green portion, cut in half lengthwise

DRESSING:

2 chipotles in adobo sauce, puréed
1 cup plain yogurt
24 large seedless green grapes

Chipotle-Lover's Chicken Salad

YOU CAN USE CANNED COOKED CHICKEN from the supermarket for this salad, but if you really want to get rave reviews for this dish, use the following method to cook the chicken breasts.

To prepare the chicken, place the chicken breasts in a glass or stainless steel bowl and cover with cold water. Add approximately 2 tablespoons of salt and let sit for an hour. Drain the chicken and put it in a medium saucepan. Add the bay leaves, garlic, parsley, and wine. Add enough water to cover the chicken and bring to a boil over medium-high heat. Reduce the heat, cover, and simmer over medium-low for 20 minutes or until the chicken is cooked through.

Remove the chicken from the pan. Rinse off any of the vegetables clinging to the chicken and discard. Place the chicken in a glass bowl, cover with plastic wrap, and refrigerate for at least 2 hours.

To make the salad, cut the chilled chicken into cubes. Put the chicken cubes, celery, parsley, green grapes, and cashews in a medium bowl and lightly mix. In a separate bowl, mix the chipotle powder, garlic, salt, and mayonnaise. Stir the mayonnaise mixture into the chicken mixture until everything is well coated. Refrigerate for at least 1 hour. Add more mayonnaise if needed for desired consistency.

When ready to serve, place 2 lettuce leaves on each of 4 individual salad plates and spoon the chicken salad on top. Garnish each chicken salad with grape halves and serve immediately.
Makes 4 Servings

CHICKEN:
4   boneless, skinless chicken breasts
2   tablespoons kosher salt
2   bay leaves
1   clove garlic, peeled
2   tablespoons fresh parsley, chopped, or 1 teaspoon dried parsley
1   cup dry white wine

SALAD:
2   large ribs celery, strings removed and finely chopped
2   tablespoons fresh parsley, chopped
1   cup seedless green grapes, cut in half
1/2 cup cashews, coarsely chopped
1/2 teaspoon chipotle powder
1/2 teaspoon granulated garlic or garlic powder
1/2 teaspoon salt
1/2 cup mayonnaise
8   green leaf, or iceberg lettuce leaves, washed and dried
Seedless green grapes, cut in half

GRiLLeD CHicKeN fajita saLaD

EVERYONE SEEMS TO LIKE FAJITAS; however, if you want the taste but don't want to do a full-blown fajita presentation, this salad is just the ticket.

Trim any excess fat from the chicken breasts and place them in a glass or stainless steel bowl. Sprinkle the kosher salt over the chicken breasts, cover with water, and let stand for 30 to 45 minutes.

Preheat a grill to medium-high. In a small bowl, mix the cumin, black pepper, and chipotle powder. Set aside.

Drain the chicken and rinse under cold running water. Pat dry with paper towels and place in a shallow bowl or dish. Coat the breasts with 2 tablespoons of the olive oil, and then sprinkle with the chipotle mixture. Turn to coat well.

Oil a rack and place over the grill. Grill the chicken for 4 to 5 minutes on each side or until cooked through. Lightly brush the bell pepper halves with olive oil and grill for 4 to 5 minutes on each side or until the skin has softened and they are nicely browned but not burned.

Take the chicken and peppers off the grill and cut into strips. Place in a medium bowl. Stir in the remaining 2 tablespoons of olive oil, onion slices, tomatoes, cilantro, lime juice, and rice vinegar. Lightly toss. Place 2 lettuce leaves on each of 4 individual salad plates and spoon the salad on top. Serve with warm, buttered tortillas on the side.

Makes 4 Servings

- 4 boneless, skinless chicken breasts
- 2 tablespoons kosher salt
- 1 teaspoon ground cumin
- 1 teaspoon freshly ground black pepper
- 1 teaspoon chipotle powder
- 5 tablespoons extra virgin olive oil
- 1 red bell pepper, cut in half and seeded
- 1 yellow bell pepper, cut in half and seeded
- 1 green bell pepper, cut in half and seeded
- 1 medium yellow onion, thinly sliced
- 4 medium, red plum tomatoes, cut lengthwise into thin slices
- 1/4 cup fresh cilantro, chopped
- Juice of 1 lime
- 2 tablespoons rice vinegar
- 8 lettuce leaves

composed sweet pepper and steak salad with chipotle-mustard vinaigrette

THIS IS AN ELEGANT SALAD. It is also an economical salad, because along with tasting great, it only uses two filet mignons for four people.

I know a lot of people on diets who cut out salad dressing altogether. I find that by using good extra virgin olive oil and cutting down on the amount of dressing you spoon over a salad, you can still enjoy the dressing without feeling so deprived.

To prepare the steaks, remove one of the chipotles from the can and reserve for the vinaigrette. Coarsely chop the rest of the chipotles. Rub the chipotles with the adobo sauce onto the top, bottom, and sides of the steaks. Let the steaks sit at room temperature for 10 to 15 minutes, turning a couple of times to make sure they are well coated with the chipotles and adobo sauce. Grill the steaks to the desired doneness. Let cool to room temperature.

To make the chipotle-mustard dressing, place all the dressing ingredients, except the oil, in a food processor and pulse until smooth. Scrape down the bowl with a rubber spatula, turn on the machine again, and add the oil in a slow, steady stream through the tube in the top. Process until well blended.

To make the salad, slice the steaks as thin as you can. Divide the head of lettuce into 4 portions and place equal amounts of lettuce on 4 individual plates. Arrange the rings of red and yellow bell pepper and the slices of filet mignon over the lettuce. Top with the red onion slices. Pour the vinaigrette over the salads. Sprinkle with grated Romano or Parmesan cheese and serve. *Makes 4 Servings*

SALAD:
- 1 (7-ounce) can chipotle in adobo sauce, rinsed and coarsely chopped
- 2 (6-ounce) filet mignons
- 1 head of leaf lettuce, leaves washed and separated
- 1 large red bell pepper, seeded and sliced into rings
- 1 large yellow bell pepper, seeded and sliced into rings
- 1 medium red onion, cut in half and thinly sliced

Romano or Parmesan cheese, grated

DRESSING:
- 1 chipotle in adobo sauce, rinsed and chopped
- 1 tablespoon Dijon mustard
- 2 cloves garlic
- $\frac{1}{2}$ teaspoon salt
- $\frac{1}{2}$ teaspoon freshly ground black pepper
- 4 tablespoons extra virgin olive oil

soups & stews

Most southwestern soups and stews use ingredients that are readily available and indigenous to this region. The authentic soups included in this chapter run the gamut from elegant starters for holiday dinners to one-dish, hearty meals—and no matter how or when they are served, these soups and stews are the essence of comfort.

TORTILLA SOUP

CRAB AND CORN CHOWDER

BOLD 'N' SPICY CATFISH SOUP

BLACK BEAN SOUP

SOUTHWESTERN PUMPKIN SOUP

CHICKEN, CHIPOTLE, AND CORN SOUP

HAPPY HOLIDAY POSOLE

A BOWL OF RED

SUPER BOWL SOUP

tortilla soup

IT IS A MEXICAN TRADITION to fry day-old corn tortillas in oil just until crisp and then use them to create a pot of delectable tortilla soup. Many cooks also add roasted green chiles or jalapeños for added heat and flavor.

In my version of this authentic soup, I often use tortilla chips when I don't have leftover tortillas, and I always add chipotle, which offers a wonderful, rich, earthy taste that makes this soup particularly satisfying on a cold winter day.

Sauté the onion and the garlic in the olive oil until soft. Spoon the onion and garlic into a blender with the tomatoes, chipotles, and 1 cup of the chicken broth. Blend until smooth. Pour the mixture into a saucepan. Stir in the rest of the chicken broth, the cooked chicken, the cilantro, and the salt. Cook over low heat for 30 minutes or until heated through.

Place the coarsely crumbled corn tortillas or tortilla chips on the bottom of individual soup bowls, pour the soup over the chips, sprinkle with cheese and olives, and serve.
Makes 4 to 6 Servings

3 tablespoons extra virgin olive oil
1 yellow onion, chopped
1 clove garlic, minced
2 large, ripe tomatoes, peeled and coarsely chopped
3 chipotles in adobo sauce
6 cups chicken broth
2 whole skinless, boneless chicken breasts, cooked and cut into bite-size pieces
1 tablespoon fresh cilantro, chopped
1/2 teaspoon kosher salt
2 cups corn tortillas, fried and coarsely crumbled, or tortilla chips, coarsely crumbled
1/2 cup Monterey Jack cheese, grated
1 cup black olives, sliced

CRAB AND CORN CHOWDER

THE SECRET TO THIS colorful soup is using good, fresh ingredients. If you have a farmer's market nearby, try to get freshly picked corn and cut the kernels off yourself. It's easy! Remove the husk and most of the silk from the corn, and then run the cob under cold water to get the remaining silk off. When the ear is clean, hold it vertically over a chopping board and, using a sharp knife, start at the middle of the ear and cut the kernels off using a swift downward motion. Try to get as close to the cob as possible. When one end is finished, reverse the ear and remove the rest of the corn.

If you can't get fresh corn, you can use frozen corn. Try to find white corn for this recipe, as it has a nice delicate flavor.

Heat 3 tablespoons of the olive oil in a large skillet. Sauté the onions, red bell pepper, and green bell pepper for 5 to 6 minutes, or until soft and tender. Heat the remaining 2 tablespoons of oil in a large saucepan or soup pot, stir in the flour, and cook over medium-high heat, stirring with a whisk until the flour is lightly browned. Rapidly stir in the chicken broth, whisking vigorously until smooth, and then whisk in the milk.

Stir in the garlic, corn, chipotle, cumin, white pepper, and bay leaves and cook, over medium heat, for 15 minutes. Gently stir in the crabmeat, parsley, and salt and cook for another 10 minutes. Remove the bay leaves and discard. Spoon into individual bowls and serve hot. *Makes 4 to 6 Servings*

5 tablespoons extra virgin olive oil
1 medium white onion, chopped
1 large red bell pepper, seeded and chopped
1 medium green bell pepper, seeded and chopped
2 tablespoons all-purpose flour
2 cups chicken broth
4 cups milk
1 clove garlic, minced
3 cups white corn, cut from the cob
   (approximately 6 ears of corn)
1 chipotle in adobo sauce, finely diced
1 teaspoon ground cumin
1/2 teaspoon ground white pepper
2 bay leaves
2 cups cooked crabmeat, picked over, rinsed
   under cold water, and shredded
2 tablespoons fresh parsley, chopped
1/2 teaspoon salt

bold 'n' spicy catfish soup

MARK TWAIN ONCE SAID, "The catfish is a plenty good enough fish for anyone." It seems his sentiment has been taken to heart by millions of Americans, as catfish is now extremely popular. But, you don't have to fry it to enjoy it. From Italian style to blackened Cajun, there are a variety of ways to enjoy catfish. This soup with its spicy flavor makes a great, easy dinner.

Heat the oil in a large saucepan or medium soup pot and sauté the onion and the garlic for 3 to 4 minutes or until soft. Add the roasted bell pepper, tomato, cumin, oregano, bay leaf, fish or chicken broth, lime juice, and chipotle powder. Bring to a boil and cook, covered, over medium heat for approximately 10 minutes.

Add the catfish and the wine and simmer over low heat for another 15 minutes or until the catfish is cooked through. Remove the bay leaf and discard. Ladle the hot soup into individual bowls. Garnish each with a couple sprigs of cilantro and serve with cornbread. *Makes 4 to 6 Servings*

2 tablespoons extra virgin olive oil
1 medium yellow onion, coarsely chopped
2 cloves garlic, minced
1 large red bell pepper, roasted, seeded, and chopped
2 large ripe tomatoes, peeled and chopped
$\frac{1}{4}$ teaspoon ground cumin
$\frac{1}{2}$ teaspoon ground oregano
1 bay leaf
6 cups fish broth or chicken broth
Juice of 1 lime
$\frac{1}{2}$ teaspoon chipotle powder
1 pound catfish filets, boned and cut into 2-inch pieces
$\frac{1}{3}$ cup dry white wine
8 sprigs fresh cilantro

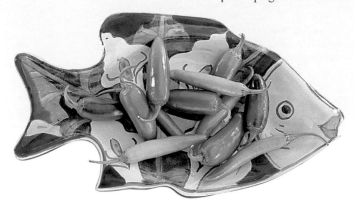

bLack bean soup

THE ONCE HUMBLE BEAN is being rediscovered and is a star in today's culinary world. Not too many years ago, you were lucky to find three or four different kinds of dried beans in the supermarket. Now there is a wide selection of both fresh and dried beans in most stores. One of the most popular beans is the black bean, which is suddenly appearing on the menus of chic restaurants from Maine to California.

Heat the oil in a medium soup pot and sauté the onions, celery, bell pepper, and carrots over medium heat for 3 to 4 minutes or until the vegetables have just started to soften. Stir in the chipotle and parsley and cook for another 2 to 3 minutes.

Add the drained beans, the chicken or vegetable broth, and the ham. Reduce the heat and simmer, covered, for approximately 20 to 30 minutes or until the vegetables are tender. Just before serving, add the lime juice. Pour into individual soup bowls and garnish each with a few thin slices of jicama. Serve immediately. *Makes 4 to 6 Servings*

2   tablespoons extra virgin olive oil
1   medium yellow onion, chopped
2   ribs celery, strings removed and chopped
1   green bell pepper, seeded and chopped
1   cup carrots, sliced
2   chipotles in adobo sauce, finely diced
2   tablespoons fresh parsley, chopped
2   (15-ounce) cans black beans, drained
5   cups chicken broth or vegetable broth
$\frac{1}{4}$ pound cooked ham, chopped
Juice of 1 lime
Approximately $\frac{1}{2}$ jicama, thinly sliced

southwestern pumpkin soup

A WIDE VARIETY OF PUMPKINS grow well in the Southwest, and long before the arrival of the Spanish, pumpkinseeds were finely ground and used to thicken dishes. Soups and stews using pumpkin were also a part of the southwestern diet even before food magazines declared them de rigueur for Thanksgiving dinner. This version is guaranteed to warm your guests and bring cheer to any occasion.

Put the peeled pumpkin pieces and the bay leaves in a large heavy pot or Dutch oven. Pour enough water over the pumpkin to completely cover it. Bring to a boil, cover, and reduce the heat to medium. Cook for 45 minutes or until the pumpkin is soft but not mushy. Remove the pumpkin from the heat, drain, and let cool. Remove the bay leaves and discard.

In a separate heavy soup pot, heat the oil, add the onion, and cook over low heat for 3 to 4 minutes or just until soft. Add the garlic and chipotle and cook for another 1 to 2 minutes.

Put the pumpkin and onion mixture in a blender or food processor. Pour in 1 cup of the chicken broth and blend until smooth. Pour the mixture back into the soup pot and add the rest of the chicken broth, the salt, and the nutmeg. Cook over low heat, stirring occasionally, until warmed through.

Ladle the soup into individual bowls, top with a spoonful of sour cream, and sprinkle a little fresh parsley on top. Serve immediately. *Makes 4 to 6 Servings*

1	pound uncooked pumpkin, peeled and cut into pieces
2	bay leaves, broken in half
2	tablespoons extra virgin olive oil
1	medium yellow onion, chopped
2	cloves garlic, minced
2	chipotles, stems removed, seeded, and finely chopped
6	cups chicken broth
$1/2$	teaspoon kosher salt
$1/4$	teaspoon ground nutmeg
Sour cream	
2	tablespoons fresh parsley, chopped

chicken, chipotle, and corn soup

ROASTING TOMATOES HELPS give recipes, including this one, a unique earthy flavor. There are two easy ways to roast tomatoes. The first way is to line a heavy cast iron skillet with aluminum foil and heat over medium-high heat. Place the tomatoes on the foil and roast them, turning several times, until they are blackened, blistered, and soft. This will take approximately 10 minutes.

The second way is to roast the tomatoes in the oven. Line a baking sheet with aluminum foil and place the tomatoes on it. Put the baking sheet approximately 4 to 5 inches under a very hot broiler. Roast them for about 5 minutes on one side and, using tongs, turn them over and roast for another 5 minutes or until blackened. After using either method, let the tomatoes cool, remove the skins, and reserve all the juice.

Heat the oil in a large saucepan or medium soup pot. Stir in the onion and sauté for 2 to 3 minutes over medium heat. Add the garlic, corn, oregano, and sage. Sauté for 2 to 3 more minutes. Add the chipotles, tomatoes, and diced chicken and continue cooking for another 2 to 3 minutes.

Pour in the chicken broth and stir. Add the salt and heat over low heat for 15 to 20 minutes or until hot. Pour the soup into individual soup bowls and garnish each with a sprinkle of white Cheddar cheese. Serve immediately.

Makes 4 to 6 Servings

- 2 tablespoons extra virgin olive oil
- 1 medium yellow onion, chopped
- 1 clove garlic, minced
- 3 cups white or yellow corn, cut off the cob, or 1 (16-ounce) package frozen corn
- $\frac{1}{2}$ teaspoon dried oregano
- $\frac{1}{2}$ teaspoon dried sage
- 2 chipotles in adobo sauce, finely diced
- 2 large, ripe tomatoes, roasted, peeled, and chopped
- 2 cups boneless chicken breasts, cooked and diced
- 6 cups chicken broth
- $\frac{1}{2}$ teaspoon salt
- 2 tablespoons white Cheddar cheese, shredded

THERE ARE A LOT OF SOUTHWEST RESIDENTS who feel that winter holiday celebrations are not complete without a bowl of posole. This traditional southwestern dish, like so many dishes handed down from generation to generation, has as many variations as there are cooks. Some folks put red chile in the posole, while others make a red chile sauce that is served on the side. This version follows the second variation so that everyone can choose his or her own amount of spiciness.

Heat the olive oil in a large soup pot. Sauté the onion for 2 to 3 minutes. Add the garlic and the ground pork and cook, stirring occasionally, until the ground pork is browned and cooked through. Stir in the oregano, cumin, and bay leaves. Then add the wine, water, hominy (with the liquid), green chiles, and the chipotle. Cook over low heat for at least 1 hour.

When ready to serve, remove and discard the bay leaves. Put the posole in a crock or in a bowl placed over a warming tray and let everybody ladle it into bowls. Serve Chipotle Red Sauce (recipe on page 94) on the side so that each person can add the desired amount of heat to their posole. Enjoy!

Makes 10 to 12 Servings

- 2 tablespoons extra virgin olive oil
- 1 large yellow onion, chopped
- 3 cloves garlic, minced
- 1 ½ pounds pork loin, coarsely ground
- 1 teaspoon dried oregano, crushed
- 2 teaspoons ground cumin
- 2 bay leaves
- 1 cup dry white wine
- 2 cups water
- 1 (6 ½-pound) can white hominy, with the liquid
- 2 medium New Mexico or Anaheim green chiles, roasted, peeled, seeded, and coarsely chopped
- 1 chipotle, finely chopped

a BOWL of RED

IN THE SOUTHWEST, a Bowl of Red is another name for chili. And, in true western-style, each bowl of chili is going to be different. You will find that people use a wide variety of chiles in order to create their own taste and their own level of heat. Also, you'll find chili made with ground beef, which is the most well-known ingredient, but also with ground pork, cubed beef, or more exotic meat such as buffalo, deer, and even elk.

This chili calls for chuck steak or pork loin, but feel free to experiment with whatever kind of meat you like. As for the heat level, this chili is HOT! The amount of chile used below is just a guideline—you can adjust it according to your own heat tolerance.

Heat the oil in a large heavy soup pot or Dutch oven and sauté the onion and garlic for 3 to 4 minutes. Stir in the meat and cook, stirring occasionally, for 4 to 5 minutes or until the meat is lightly browned. Add the rest of the ingredients and bring to a boil over high heat. Reduce the heat to low and simmer for 1 hour, stirring occasionally.

Ladle the chili into individual serving bowls, and serve with warm flour tortillas, cold beer, and watermelon for dessert.

Makes 6 to 8 Servings

*Mexican chocolate is made with cinnamon. There are two or three brands usually available in most supermarkets or in stores specializing in Mexican and Latin American cuisine. If you are unable to find it, substitute shaved semi-sweet chocolate and add a pinch of cinnamon.

2	tablespoons extra virgin olive oil
1	large yellow onion, finely chopped
3	cloves garlic, finely minced
2	pounds chuck steak or pork loin, cut into 1-inch pieces
8	large ripe tomatoes, peeled and diced, or 2 (14 1/2-ounce) cans diced tomatoes
1	(7-ounce) can chipotle in adobo sauce, puréed
2	tablespoons New Mexico red chile powder
1	ounce Mexican chocolate, shaved*
6	cups water
1	teaspoon ground cumin
1	teaspoon dried cilantro, crushed
1	teaspoon ground oregano
1	teaspoon salt

super bowl soup

ON VISITS TO WASHINGTON, D.C., my wife and I often had lunch in the Capitol building and enjoyed their famous Senate Bean Soup. We decided some time ago that while the soup was good, we could improve upon it—so we made this version with chipotle. Amazingly, it has become such a hit with family and friends that now we serve it at our annual Super Bowl Sunday celebration. This soup is just the ticket for a fun and festive gathering.

In a heavy soup pot or Dutch oven, heat the oil and sauté the onions and garlic for 2 to 3 minutes. Add the celery with the tops, the carrots, parsley flakes, and chipotle. Stir and heat through. Add the beans and chicken broth. Bring to a boil and then reduce the heat to low. Simmer for about 1 hour. Add salt to taste, if desired.

Place the soup in a crock and surround it with bowls, spoons, etc. Serve it with good fresh French bread and butter or ham salad sandwiches.

For the more daring in your group, serve a bowl of Chipotle Red Sauce (recipe on page 94) on the side, and let each person add the desired amount to their soup.

Makes 4 to 6 Servings

2 tablespoons extra virgin olive oil
1 medium yellow onion, minced
1 clove garlic, minced
2 ribs celery with the tops, strings removed and chopped
$^1/_2$ cup carrots, chopped into small chunks
1 teaspoon dry parsley flakes
3 chipotles in adobo sauce, puréed
3 (15-ounce) cans great northern beans, drained
6 cups chicken broth
Salt to taste

entrées

When you're asked the perennial question, "what's for dinner?" make it easy on yourself and pick from one of these entrées. Whether you're in the mood for seafood, pork, chicken, or beef, these zippy chipotle dishes, many of them variations on traditional comfort food, will turn "what's for dinner?" into "let's have this again—soon!"

beef

BEEF SALPICÓN WITH CHIPOTLE DRESSING
FOLDED SOFT TACOS AL CARBÓN
MEATBALLS DIABLO
BARBECUED BEEF BRISKET
WHOA-COWBOY STEAKS

chicken

CHICKEN BREAST ROSADO
TANGERINE CHICKEN
BROILED CHICKEN WITH CHIPOTLE-
   TARRAGON MARINADE
SMOTHERED CHICKEN

pork

PORK MEDALLIONS WITH PAPAYA-TEQUILA SAUCE
HAM AND POTATO SCALLOP
PORK ROAST WITH PIZZAZZ!

seafood

SALMON STEAKS WITH CHIPOTLE MUSTARD
BAKED HALIBUT WITH CHIPOTLE MAYONNAISE
CRAB, AVOCADO, AND PAPAYA ENCHILADAS
CRAB TOSTADAS
GRILLED SHRIMP MARINATED IN LIME AND CHIPOTLE
SHRIMP CEVICHE
SAUTÉED SHRIMP WITH CHIPOTLE AND TEQUILA
SWEET, SMOKY GRILLED SHRIMP

beef salpicón with chipotle dressing

SALPICÓN, OR SALMAGUNDI as it is otherwise known, is a cold, salad-like main dish of chopped meat, poultry, or seafood mixed with onions, oil, and spices. This is a great choice for a summer lunch or as the main course for a light buffet dinner. Be aware that this recipe takes two days to prepare, so plan ahead. It will be well worth the effort!

The day before you plan to serve the salpicón, prepare the brisket. Start by preheating the oven to 400° F. Place the brisket in a large baking pan, trim off any excess fat, sprinkle a package of prepared onion soup mix over the brisket, and rub it into the meat. Cover the brisket with the champagne or white wine and the water. Cover the pan tightly with aluminum foil and bake for one hour. Reduce the heat to 300° F. and continue cooking for 3 to 4 hours or until the brisket is cooked through. Remove the brisket from the pan and place it in a non-reactive bowl. Refrigerate overnight.

The next day, prepare the salpicón. Start by shredding the brisket and cutting it into pieces approximately 2 to 3 inches long. Place the shredded brisket in a large mixing bowl.

In a separate small bowl, mix all of the dressing ingredients together. Pour the dressing over the meat and toss to make sure the dressing coats all of the meat. (I find the best way to do this is with your hands). Put the mixture in the refrigerator for at least 1 hour.

Line a shallow bowl or platter with the lettuce and mound the meat on top. Sprinkle the chopped olives and onions on top of the meat and place the tomato wedges around the sides of the meat. Serve with a pasta salad and Mexican rolls on the side.

Makes 6 to 8 Servings

BRISKET:

4-6 pounds cold beef brisket
1 (2-ounce) package onion soup mix
2 cups champagne or white wine
2 cups water

DRESSING:

4 tablespoons extra virgin olive oil
3 tablespoons balsamic vinegar
3 tablespoons rice vinegar
2 tablespoons fresh lemon juice
3 cloves garlic, minced or squeezed
  through a garlic press
3 chipotles in adobo sauce, minced
2 tablespoons fresh cilantro, chopped
1/2 teaspoon salt

SALPICÓN:

8-10 lettuce leaves
1/2 cup green pimento-stuffed olives, chopped
4-6 green onions, with the white parts and
  some of the green parts, chopped
3 medium, ripe tomatoes, cut into wedges

folded soft tacos al carbón

ALTHOUGH GROUND BEEF is currently the ubiquitous filling in most tacos, we still prefer to make them with thinly sliced grilled steak—al carbón. The warm steak enveloped in a super-fresh flour tortilla topped with red onion, tomatoes, cilantro, and a delicate avocado salsa makes these tacos número uno!

Prepare the chipotle rub, and place it in a shallow bowl. Putting one steak in the bowl at a time, rub and press the spices all over the steak until it is well coated. Grill the steaks to the desired doneness. Let stand for 5 minutes, and then thinly slice each steak across the grain.

Preheat the oven to 300° F. Wet a clean tea towel and lay half of it in a shallow baking pan large enough to hold the tortillas. Place the tortillas on the towel, fold it over to cover them, and heat in the oven for 10 minutes or until the tortillas have steamed through and are warm. Or, you can heat the tortillas, one or two at a time, in a microwave on high for 15 to 30 seconds or until they are warm.

Divide the steak pieces into 12 equal portions and place each portion on one half of each tortilla. Top with some of the red onion, tomato, and cilantro. Drizzle approximately 1 tablespoon of the Avocado and Jicama Salsa over the top, fold the tortillas, and serve with pinto beans, Spanish rice, and a green salad. *Makes 6 Servings*

Chipotle Rub (recipe on page 92)
2   pounds rib-eye steaks (approximately
    3-4 steaks, each 1 $\frac{1}{2}$-inches thick)
12 (6-inch) flour tortillas
1   medium red onion, sliced very thin
4   ripe tomatoes, peeled, seeded, and chopped
1   tablespoon fresh cilantro, chopped
Avocado and Jicama Salsa (recipe on page 90)

meatballs diablo

I CAN'T REMEMBER a world without meatballs. When we were kids, we clamored for meatballs and spaghetti, and at Christmastime, my favorite aunt and her Swedish husband served meatballs swimming in a rich cream sauce. However, when I lived in Spain, I quickly learned that meatballs were not relegated to those two dishes. I soon discovered that they are absolutely splendid in soup and are also delicious when served in a spicy sauce over rice. Even though one restaurant owner gave me his recipe, I never could duplicate it when I got back to the States, so I made up my own using chipotle in adobo sauce. I like to call it the Devil's Meatballs.

Heat the olive oil in a large skillet and cook the onion until soft but not browned. Mix the ground beef and ground pork together in a mixing bowl and stir in the onions. In a separate bowl, lightly beat the eggs, and then slowly add them to the meat mixture. Add the chipotle, bread crumbs, cumin, garlic, nutmeg, and parsley. Mix well and form into balls approximately the size of walnuts. Place on a plate or platter until ready to cook.

Heat the vegetable oil in the same skillet you used for the onions, and sauté the meatballs until well browned and cooked through. Use these meatballs in your favorite vegetable soup or serve them as an appetizer with a prepared barbecue sauce or Chipotle Barbecue Sauce (see recipe on page 92).
Makes 4 to 6 Servings

2 tablespoons extra virgin olive oil
1 medium yellow onion, finely chopped
1 pound lean ground beef
1 pound ground pork
2 eggs
2 chipotles in adobo sauce, puréed
1 cup unseasoned bread crumbs
$^1\!/_2$ teaspoon ground cumin
1 clove garlic, minced
$^1\!/_2$ teaspoon ground nutmeg
2 tablespoons fresh parsley, chopped, or 1 teaspoon dried parsley
$^1\!/_4$ cup vegetable oil

barbecued beef brisket

IN OUR PART OF THE WORLD everybody serves barbecued brisket. The trick to making the perfect brisket is to cook it until it is very tender, let it cool, refrigerate it for at least eight hours, and then slice it up beautifully. Be aware that it generally takes two days to make this recipe, so cook the brisket the day before you plan to serve it.

There are several good bottled barbecue sauces on the market if you're short on time; however, we prefer making our own. Instead of using chili powder or cayenne, we're crazy about chipotle and think that it adds just the right amount of heat and smoke. Give it a try!

The day before you plan to serve this dish, preheat the oven to 400° F. Place the brisket in a large roasting pan. (I line the pan with aluminum foil to help the clean up process.) Mix the remaining ingredients, except for the barbecue sauce, in a medium bowl. Pour the mixture over the brisket. Cover with heavy-duty aluminum foil, seal the edges, and bake for 1 hour. Turn the heat down to 325° F. and continue to cook for 4 hours. After 4 hours, carefully remove the foil and check the brisket. If it is starting to dry out, carefully add more beer or water. Reseal with the aluminum foil and continue to cook for 1 to 2 more hours or until the brisket is tender.

Let the brisket cool, take it out of the juice, wrap it in foil, and refrigerate overnight. Discard the juice.

The next day, preheat the oven to 350° F. Take the brisket out of the refrigerator, slice it across the grain, and place the slices in a large flat pan. Ladle the Chipotle Barbecue Sauce over the slices and warm it in the oven until just warmed through, approximately 15 minutes. Serve immediately. *Makes 8 to 12 Servings*

1 (10-pound) beef brisket, trimmed of excess fat
1 (7-ounce) can chipotle in adobo sauce, puréed
2 (12-ounce) bottles dark beer such as Negra Modelo
1 cup Worcestershire sauce
1/2 cup soy sauce
1/2 cup dried onions, minced
1 tablespoon granulated garlic
Chipotle Barbecue Sauce
(recipe on page 92)

WHOa-cowboy steaks

WE LIVE IN THE HEART of cattle country and even though the local cowboys and ranchers use computers and sell their cattle on cable television, some of the old customs still survive. They still use horses to check for breaks in the fence and to round up stray cattle. They still have ropings to hone their skills, and they still love their steaks. One of their favorite methods of preparation is to take a hearty steak, dip it in a flour-cornmeal batter, and then fry it. The result is absolutely delicious!

Combine the eggs and water in a medium bowl. Set aside. In another medium bowl, mix together the cornmeal, flour, salt, chipotle powder, garlic powder, and paprika. Set aside.

Pound the steaks with a meat tenderizer until they are at least a $\frac{1}{4}$-inch thick and the fibers are soft. Dip the steaks into the egg mixture and coat both sides. Then dip them into the cornmeal mixture and completely coat them. Place them on a plate until all the steaks are coated.

Heat $\frac{1}{2}$-inch of oil in a cast iron skillet. Carefully place the steaks in the oil and let cook until browned on one side. Carefully turn over and brown the other side. Drain on paper towels before serving. These steaks are great when served with Avocado and Jicama Salsa, pinto beans, and coleslaw. *Makes 4 Servings*

2　large eggs, lightly beaten
2　tablespoons water
1　cup cornmeal
1　cup all-purpose flour
1　teaspoon salt
2　teaspoons chipotle powder
1　teaspoon garlic powder
1　tablespoon paprika
4　boneless top round steaks,
　　cut $\frac{1}{2}$-inch thick
Oil for frying
Avocado and Jicama Salsa
　(recipe on page 90)

chicken breast rosado

ROSADO MEANS "ROSY" or "rose-colored" in Spanish, and this dish lives up to its name. The chipotle in adobo sauce not only turns the sauce pink but also gives the chicken a deep rich, spicy flavor.

Preheat the oven to 350° F. Place the chicken breasts in a stainless steel or glass bowl. Sprinkle the kosher salt over them and cover with water. Let stand for 30 minutes. Remove the breasts from the bowl and rinse thoroughly.

Pour the olive oil in a medium baking pan. Stir the paprika into the oil. Put the chicken breasts in the pan and coat with the oil and paprika. Bake the chicken for 20 minutes.

Mix the yogurt and grapefruit juice together. Stir the minced chipotle with a little adobo sauce into the yogurt and grapefruit juice mixture. Stir in the cumin, cilantro, and white pepper and pour the yogurt mixture over the chicken breasts. Return the chicken to the oven and bake for another 15 minutes or until the chicken is done and the sauce is hot and bubbly. Remove the chicken from the pan. Place each piece of chicken on a plate and spoon the sauce over the chicken. Garnish with the almonds.

This chicken is especially good when served over rice in which you have stirred a ½ cup of cooked green peas. *Makes 4 Servings*

4 boneless, skinless chicken breasts
1 tablespoon kosher salt
1 tablespoon extra virgin olive oil
2 teaspoons paprika
1 cup plain yogurt
½ cup pink grapefruit juice
2 chipotles in adobo sauce, minced
1 teaspoon ground cumin
1 tablespoon fresh cilantro, chopped
½ teaspoon ground white pepper
⅓ cup sliced almonds

tangerine chicken

MOST CHINESE RESTAURANTS serve Lemon Chicken and/or Orange Chicken. However, Tangerine Chicken is harder to come by, so we always end up making our own. Years ago, we used pequín chiles for the heat factor, but more recently, we switched to chipotle chiles, as the smoky heat is a great complement to the sweetness of the tangerines.

Heat the oil in an ovenproof pan and sauté the onion, the grated peel from two of the tangerines, the garlic, and the chipotle over medium heat for 4 to 5 minutes. Reduce the heat, add the tangerine juice and the wine, and simmer for 10 minutes.

Preheat the oven to 325° F. Put the chicken breasts in the pan with the sauce, making sure that each breast is well-coated, cover, and bake for 15 minutes. Remove the cover, add the bell pepper, and bake for an additional 15 minutes. Remove the chicken to a warm platter, spoon the sauce over the chicken, and garnish with the remaining grated tangerine peel. Serve on a mound of brown or refried rice.

Makes 4 Servings

2 tablespoons extra virgin olive oil
$^{1}/_{2}$ medium yellow onion, chopped
Peel from 3 tangerines, grated (use only the colored part as the white part tends to be bitter)
1 clove garlic, minced
1-2 chipotles, stems removed and finely diced
2 cups fresh tangerine juice
3 tablespoons dry white wine
4 boneless, skinless chicken breasts
1 medium green bell pepper, seeded and coarsely chopped

BROILED CHICKEN WITH CHIPOTLE-TARRAGON MARINADE

TARRAGON AND CHICKEN ARE one of those natural pairings like cheese and wine. However, when we added chipotle to a marinade with tarragon, it elevated this dish to super-star status.

Place the chicken breasts in a shallow glass bowl. In a separate bowl, mix together the rest of the ingredients, pour over the chicken, and marinate in the refrigerator for 1 hour.

Remove the chicken from the marinade and reserve the marinade. Grill the chicken for 2 to 3 minutes on each side or until done, continually basting with the marinade. Discard the remaining marinade. Slice the chicken on the diagonal and serve with your favorite stir-fried vegetables. *Makes 6 to 8 Servings*

6 boneless, skinless chicken breasts
1 teaspoon dried tarragon, crushed
4 green onions, with some of the green portion, chopped
1 cup dry (French) vermouth
2 cloves garlic, cut in half and crushed
$\frac{1}{2}$ teaspoon chipotle powder

WE USE A LOT OF CANNED CHIPOTLES in adobo sauce. However, as with any canned product, making your own adobo sauce is better. This rich, red sauce made with chile, vinegar, tomatoes, garlic, and onion is perfect for roasting or grilling chicken breasts, or use it, as in this recipe, to smother and cook chicken in a slow cooker to give it a deep, smoky southwestern flavor.

Place the chicken breasts in a non-reactive bowl, sprinkle with kosher salt, and cover with water. Let stand for 30 minutes, rinse under cold running water, and pat dry. Set aside.

Place the chipotles and the New Mexico chiles in a glass bowl and cover with the vinegar, water, and wine. Let stand for 10 minutes. Place the mixture in a blender and add the tomatoes, garlic, oregano, cumin, salt, and black pepper. Blend until almost smooth.

Heat the olive oil in a skillet and sauté the onion for 3 to 4 minutes. Spoon the onions into a slow cooker and add the chicken breasts, the chile mixture, and the bay leaves. Cover and cook on high for 1 hour. Reduce the heat to low and cook for 4 to 5 hours or until the chicken is tender. Remove the bay leaves and discard. Place each chicken breast on a plate, top with a little adobo sauce from the slow cooker, and serve with polenta and a fresh green salad.

Makes 4 Servings

4   boneless, skinless chicken breasts
1   tablespoon kosher salt
3   chipotle chiles, stems removed and chopped
3   dried red New Mexico chiles, stems and seeds removed
1/4 cup rice vinegar
1   cup water
1   cup dry white wine
2   medium ripe tomatoes, coarsely chopped
2   cloves garlic, halved
1/2 teaspoon dried oregano, crushed
1/2 teaspoon ground cumin
1/2 teaspoon kosher salt
1/2 teaspoon freshly ground black pepper
2   tablespoons extra virgin olive oil
1   medium white onion, chopped
2   bay leaves

pork medallions with papaya-tequila sauce

AS WITH SO MANY GREAT RECIPES, this one came about quite by accident. I was going to make Pork Marsala, but I couldn't find any Marsala in the house. My wife had just juiced a large, ripe papaya, and we thought, "Why don't we use some of that juice?" Then we added our old stand-by, tequila, and a truly superb dish was born.

If you can't find pork medallions in your supermarket, buy pork chops that are approximately 1-inch thick. It is better if they are boneless, but if they do have the bone, just take a sharp knife and cut the center away from the bone. Then, carefully holding the chop on one edge, butterfly it to make two medallions about $1/2$-inch thick. Finally, pound the medallions so that they are approximately $1/4$-inch thick.

Mix the flour, chipotle, salt, and garlic powder together in a shallow bowl and dredge the pork in the flour mixture. Heat the olive oil in a non-stick skillet over medium heat, and then sauté the pork for 3 to 4 minutes on each side until the medallions are lightly browned and the pork is cooked through. Do not overcook. Remove the pork to a warm platter and set aside or place in a warm, 200° F. oven.

Pour the papaya juice into the skillet and stir to deglaze the pan. Add the tequila and orange juice and cook, stirring, until the sauce reduces slightly. Stir in the butter and add a pinch or two more of the chipotle powder if desired.

Continue to cook for about 1 more minute or until the sauce is of desired consistency. Place the warm medallions on individual serving plates, pour the sauce over the medallions, and garnish each with a few sprigs of cilantro or chopped green onion. Serve immediately. Cornbread, fresh asparagus, and a light beer make the perfect accompaniments to this dish. *Makes 4 Servings*

1 cup all-purpose flour
1 teaspoon chipotle powder
$1/2$ teaspoon salt
$1/2$ teaspoon garlic powder
4 pork medallions, pounded to approximately $1/4$-inch thick
4 tablespoons extra virgin olive oil
1 cup papaya juice, fresh, canned, or frozen
$1/4$ cup gold tequila
$1/4$ cup fresh orange juice
4 tablespoons unsalted butter
Approximately 8 sprigs cilantro
2 tablespoons green onions, chopped

OPPOSITE: *Pork Medallions with Papaya-Tequila Sauce (recipe above) and Chipotle and Garlic Mashed Potatoes (recipe on page 75).*

59

ham and potato scallop

THIS IS ONE OF THOSE comfort food dishes that just keeps reinventing itself. The ritual in our house is to bake a ham, serve it sliced for a couple of meals, and then divide up the rest to use in scalloped potatoes and ham salad.

I've tried all sorts of things to give the scalloped potatoes a little more flair. Chipotle is a great addition, because the smoky heat gives this often bland dish a real wake-up call.

Preheat the oven to 350° F. Spray a 13 x 9-inch glass baking dish with vegetable spray. Layer the potato slices in the bottom of the dish, slightly overlapping each slice. Sprinkle the chopped ham over the potatoes. Sprinkle the onion slices over the ham and potatoes. Top with another layer of sliced potatoes.

Melt the butter in a large heavy skillet. Stir in the flour and lightly brown. Stir in the milk and whisk until smooth. Bring to a boil over medium-high heat and then reduce the heat to low. Stir in the paprika, garlic, chicken bouillon, parsley, and chipotle and simmer for 2 to 3 minutes.

Pour the milk mixture over the layered potatoes to cover (add more milk or half-and-half if necessary to cover the potatoes). Sprinkle the bread-crumbs and the Parmesan cheese over the top. Bake for 45 minutes to 1 hour or until bubbly and lightly browned on the top, and the potatoes test done with a fork. Serve immediately.

Makes 4 to 6 Servings

5   large white potatoes, peeled and
    thinly sliced
2   cups cooked, chopped ham
1   large yellow onion, cut in half and
    thinly sliced
4   tablespoons butter
4   tablespoons all-purpose flour
5   cups milk (or 4 cups milk and 1 cup
    half-and-half for a richer taste)
1   teaspoon paprika
1   teaspoon granulated garlic
1   teaspoon chicken bouillon granules
1   tablespoon dried parsley
2   chipotles in adobo sauce, puréed
1/2 cup Italian or unseasoned bread crumbs
1/2 cup Parmesan cheese, grated

pork roast with pizzazz!

THE FIRST MEAL I EVER COOKED for my wife was a pork loin roasted with fresh fruit and orange liqueur. I served this dish at a Christmas party she attended, and she politely ate some of it. I found out years later that she absolutely hated any kind of sweet meat. Since that time, she has taken over cooking our pork roasts, and she uses a wide variety of tasty ingredients such as garlic and soy sauce. When we were asked for an additional pork recipe for this book, we came up with this delicious pork roast with chipotle that will give any meal real pizzazz! Use caution, though, as this recipe is not for the uninitiated. It is extremely hot, so adjust the amount of chipotle to your heat tolerance.

Preheat the oven to 350° F.

Using a small, sharp knife, make 14 cuts in the pork roast about 1 ½ inches deep. Insert the garlic cloves into the cuts, spacing them out evenly so you can insert chipotle pieces between them. Carefully remove 2 of the chipotles from the can and cut each of them into 3 pieces. Using the handle of a teaspoon, insert each piece of chipotle into the remaining incisions. Place the roast in a baking pan.

Place the remaining chipotle in adobo sauce in a blender and pulse until smooth. In a measuring cup, add the appropriate amount of wine, and then stir in the blended chipotle. Pour the mixture over the pork roast, cover securely with aluminum foil, place in the oven, and bake for 1 hour. Uncover the roast, turn it over, cover it again, and continue baking it for another 30 minutes. After 30 minutes, turn the roast over again, recover, and bake for another 30 minutes or until the meat is cooked through.

Let the meat stand for 10 minutes, slice it across the grain, and place the slices on a serving platter. This meat is especially tasty when served with roasted white potatoes, roasted sweet potatoes, roasted onions, and a garnish of fresh parsley. *Makes 4 to 6 Servings*

1 pork loin roast (approximately 3 ½-pounds), rinsed and patted dry
8 small cloves garlic
1 (7-ounce) can chipotle in adobo sauce, or adjust to taste
2 cups dry white wine

salmon steaks with chipotle mustard

THE SMOKY QUALITY of the chipotle combined with the sweet tang of honey mustard creates a superlative marinade for fish. Refer to the photo on page 76 for a creative serving suggestion.

Put the yogurt, wine, honey mustard, chipotle, and chopped green onions in a food processor. Pulse until well blended. Spread the mixture on both sides of the salmon steaks and let sit, at room temperature, for 10 minutes. Place the steaks in a broiler pan and broil about 4 inches from the heat for approximately 6 minutes. Turn over and broil another 6 minutes or until done to taste. Serve with rice and a fresh spinach salad.
Makes 4 Servings

1   cup plain yogurt
$^1/_2$ cup dry white wine
1   tablespoon honey mustard
$^1/_2$ teaspoon chipotle chile powder
2   green onions, with the white part and most of the green part, coarsely chopped
4   (6-ounce) salmon steaks, skin and bones removed

baked halibut with chipotle mayonnaise

I LIKE HALIBUT! Although it's good broiled and then topped with a little butter and lemon, it becomes truly sublime when baked with white wine and topped with chipotle mayonnaise.

Preheat oven to 350° F. Put the fish in a shallow glass baking dish. In a separate bowl, mix the wine and chicken broth together. Stir in the green onions. Pour the mixture over the fish. Sprinkle the chipotle over the halibut steaks and bake for 12 to 15 minutes or until the fish flakes easily when tested with a fork.

Carefully lift the fish out of the pan with a spatula or large slotted spoon. Place the steaks on individual serving plates. Squeeze half a lemon over each steak. Top with a spoonful of soft butter and a spoonful of Chipotle Mayonnaise. Serve with steamed spinach and rice. *Makes 4 Servings*

4   (6-ounce) halibut steaks, $1/2$-inch thick
$1/2$ cup dry white wine
$1/2$ cup chicken broth
3   green onions, white portion only, sliced
$1/2$ teaspoon chipotle powder
2   medium lemons, cut in half
4   tablespoons butter, at room temperature
Chipotle Mayonnaise (recipe on page 95)

crab, avocado, and papaya enchiladas

WHEN I WAS EXECUTIVE CHEF at a Mexican café in a four-star hotel, I started experimenting with the ingredients in our chicken enchiladas. The owner of the hotel and my faithful guests thought I'd lost my mind until they got brave enough to taste this unique offering. These enchiladas turned out to be one of the guests' all-time favorite recipes.

To make the sauce, melt one tablespoon of the butter in a skillet over medium heat and sauté the onion for 3 to 4 minutes or until soft. Remove from the skillet and set aside.

Melt the rest of the butter in the skillet over medium-high heat, stir in the flour, and whisk until the flour has lightly browned. Add the milk, whisking constantly until smooth. Whisk in the bouillon and reduce the heat to medium-low. Stir in the green chiles and chipotle and cook for 2 to 3 minutes or until warm. Reduce the heat to low and keep warm while you make the enchiladas.

To make the enchiladas, preheat the oven to 350° F. Spray a 9 x 13-inch Pyrex baking dish with vegetable cooking spray. Heat the olive oil in a medium skillet and sauté the onion for 2 to 3 minutes. Add the garlic, crabmeat, cilantro, papaya, chipotle, salt, and cumin. Cook for another 2 to 3 minutes or until all the ingredients are warm.

Dip the corn tortillas, one at a time, in the warm green chile sauce and place in the prepared baking dish. Divide the crab mixture into 12 equal portions. Spoon 1 portion of the crab mixture into the center of each tortilla and fold in half. Pour the remaining green chile sauce over the enchiladas and sprinkle the Monterey Jack and Colby cheese on top. Bake for 15 minutes or until the cheese has melted and the enchiladas are heated through.

To serve, place 2 enchiladas on each of six plates. Arrange the avocado slices on top of the enchiladas. Spoon a dollop of sour cream in the center, sprinkle with sliced black olives, and garnish with a sprig of cilantro. Serve warm with refried beans and confetti rice. *Makes 6 Servings*

SAUCE:
- 3 tablespoons butter
- 1/2 medium white onion, finely chopped
- 2 tablespoons all-purpose flour
- 2 cups milk
- 1 teaspoon chicken bouillon granules
- 3 New Mexico or Anaheim green chiles, roasted, peeled, seeded, and finely chopped
- 1 chipotle in adobo sauce, finely diced

ENCHILADAS:
- 2 tablespoons extra virgin olive oil
- 1 small white onion, diced
- 2 cloves garlic, minced
- 1 pound cooked crabmeat, picked over, washed, drained, and shredded
- 1 tablespoon fresh cilantro, chopped
- 2 cups papaya, finely diced
- 2 chipotles in adobo sauce, finely chopped
- 1/4 teaspoon salt
- 1/2 teaspoon ground cumin
- 12 (6-inch) corn tortillas
- 1 cup Monterey Jack cheese, shredded
- 1 cup Colby cheese, shredded
- 2 large avocados, peeled, seeded, and sliced
- Sour Cream
- 10-12 black olives, sliced
- 6 sprigs cilantro

THIS DISH MAKES A GREAT light lunch, especially when accompanied by a green salad and your favorite beverage. If you don't want to spend the extra money for real crabmeat, you can substitute quality imitation crabmeat that is found in most supermarkets.

Place the onion, garlic, tomato, and chipotle in a food processor. Pulse just enough to coarsely chop. Add the lime juice, olive oil, olives, salt, cilantro, and crabmeat. Pulse until just blended. Do NOT purée. Set aside. To make the tostadas, cover the bottom of a 9-inch skillet with approximately ¼-inch of olive oil and heat until very hot but not smoking. Using tongs, dip the tortillas, 1 at a time, in the oil and rapidly fry until lightly browned on both sides. Drain the tortillas on paper towels. Place 2 fried tortillas on each plate and spoon the crabmeat mixture on top of each tostada. Garnish each with a sprig of cilantro and serve.
Makes 4 Servings

1　small white onion, coarsely chopped
1　clove garlic, halved
1　large firm, ripe tomato, quartered
1　chipotle, stem removed, seeded, and crushed
1　tablespoon fresh lime juice
1　tablespoon extra virgin olive oil
¼　cup olives, pitted and chopped
Pinch salt
1　tablespoon fresh cilantro, chopped
1　pound cooked crabmeat, picked over, washed, drained, and shredded
8　(6-inch) corn tortillas
8　sprigs cilantro

GRiLLeð SHRiMP MARiNAteð iN LiME AND CHIPOTLE

THE GREAT AROMA that wafts up from the bowl when you marinade this shrimp might tempt you to let it sit longer than the requisite fifteen minutes. Resist the temptation, however, as the shrimp will "cook" in the marinade if left for too long. The fresh, summery taste of the melon salsa provides an enticing counterpoint to the sharp bite of the chipotle.

To prepare the shrimp, mix the lime juice, wine, garlic, chipotle, salt, and black pepper together in a glass bowl. Stir in the shrimp and let marinate at room temperature for 15 minutes. Remove the shrimp from the marinade, discard the marinade, and grill the shrimp over medium-high heat, turning once or twice, for 5 to 6 minutes or until done. Set aside.

To prepare the melon salsa, mix all of the salsa ingredients together and refrigerate for 1 hour before serving. This salsa will not keep well for more than a few hours.

Divide the shrimp equally on 4 plates and spoon the salsa over the shrimp. This shrimp is delicious when served with oven-roasted garlic potatoes or linguine with a garlic butter sauce.
Makes 4 Servings

SHRIMP:
- $1/4$ cup fresh lime juice
- $1/2$ cup white wine
- 1 clove garlic, minced
- 1 chipotle, stem removed and chopped
- $1/2$ teaspoon salt
- $1/2$ teaspoon freshly ground black pepper
- 1 pound (16-20 count) large shrimp, peeled and deveined

SALSA:
- 1 cup cantaloupe, peeled, seeded, and diced
- 1 cup honeydew melon, peeled, seeded, and diced
- $1/2$ white onion, finely chopped
- 2 jalapeños, diced
- 2 tablespoons fresh lime juice
- 1 tablespoon fresh cilantro, chopped
- $1/2$ teaspoon kosher salt
- $1/2$ teaspoon ground cumin

shrimp ceviche

THIS DISH COMBINES the jalapeño with its dried, smoked counterpart—chipotle. The citrus juice "cooks" the shrimp, which makes a wonderful luncheon salad or could work well as an appetizer.

Select jalapeños that are dark green and firm to the touch. The secret for this dish is to chop the jalapeños very fine. Although you can use a food processor to do this, I find that the best and easiest way is to cut the jalapeños into quarters lengthwise with a sharp knife, scrape out the white membranes and seeds, line up the strips, and then finely chop them.

Place the shrimp is a glass bowl. Add the jalapeños, chipotle, onion, tomatoes, oregano, cilantro, salt, and black pepper. Pour the lime juice and lemon juice over the shrimp and mix lightly. Chill in the refrigerator for at least 4 hours, so that the shrimp can "cook" in the liquid. Arrange the lettuce leaves on individual serving plates and spoon the shrimp on top of the lettuce. Place the avocado slices around the shrimp. *Makes 4 to 6 Servings*

1   pound (30-36 count) medium shrimp, peeled and deveined
2   jalapeños, seeded, membranes removed, and finely chopped
1   chipotle in adobo sauce, rinsed and finely diced
1/2 white onion, finely chopped
2   medium ripe, firm tomatoes, diced
1   teaspoon dried Mexican oregano
1   tablespoon fresh cilantro, chopped
1/2 teaspoon kosher salt
1/2 teaspoon freshly ground black pepper
1   cup fresh lime juice
1/4 cup fresh lemon juice
1   head iceberg lettuce, washed and divided into 4 or 6 portions
1   large avocado, peeled, seeded, and cut into approximately 8-12 slices

sautéed shrimp with chipotle and tequila

SHRIMP IS SO VERSATILE and complements so many flavors that it is one of my favorite foods. Not long ago, we had two guests helping in the kitchen. They are both excellent, long-time cooks, and I was surprised when they said they had never peeled or deveined shrimp.

It is an easy procedure. You can buy an inexpensive plastic gadget that slips down the back of the shrimp, removes the shell, and deveins it in one deft motion. If you don't have one of those handy gizmos, use a small paring knife, slip it underneath the shell, loosen the shell, remove the knife, and, using your fingers, remove the shell. Then take the knife and cut a thin line on the back of the shrimp, which will reveal a black line of waste material. Using the tip of the knife, remove this black matter and then rinse the shrimp under cold, running water.

Heat the olive oil in a pan and sauté the garlic and parsley for 1 to 2 minutes. In a separate bowl, combine the flour, white pepper, salt, and chipotle powder. Lightly coat the shrimp in the flour mixture and place them in the pan with the garlic and parsley. Cook over medium heat for 5 to 7 minutes, turning once or twice, until they are just done and lightly browned. Remove the shrimp from the pan, place on an ovenproof serving platter, and set in a warm, 250° F. oven.

In the same sauté pan, pour the wine, lemon juice, and tequila, turn the heat to high, and deglaze the pan. Add the diced chipotle and the butter. Simmer for 3 to 4 minutes on medium heat until the sauce thickens slightly. Remove the shrimp from the warm oven, pour the sauce over shrimp, sprinkle toasted sesame seeds over the top, and garnish with the green onions. This dish is especially good when served over rice that has been cooked with 1 teaspoon of turmeric, which creates a delightful yellow color. *Makes 4 Servings*

4 tablespoons extra virgin olive oil
1 clove garlic, squeezed through a garlic press
1 teaspoon fresh parsley, chopped
1 cup all-purpose flour
1/2 teaspoon ground white pepper
1/2 teaspoon salt
1/2 teaspoon chipotle powder
1 pound (16-20 count) jumbo shrimp, peeled and deveined
1/2 cup dry white wine
2 tablespoons fresh lemon juice
2 tablespoons gold tequila
1 chipotle, stem removed and finely diced
4 tablespoons unsalted butter
1/4 cup toasted sesame seeds
3 green onions, with some of the green portion, finely chopped

sweet, smoky grilled shrimp

SHRIMP AND CITRUS JUICE are the perfect pairing. The addition of chipotle gives the shrimp a sweet and smoky flavor that is delicious when served with rice and a green salad.

When grilling the shrimp, use a slotted grill so that the shrimp won't fall through. Also, make sure to spray the grill with vegetable oil cooking spray so the shrimp won't stick.

Heat the olive oil in a skillet over medium heat. Sauté the onion for 4 to 5 minutes, add the garlic, cumin, and oregano and cook for 2 more minutes. Let cool slightly, and then spoon the mixture into a food processor. Add the wine, orange liqueur, and chipotle. Purée until smooth. Spoon half of the purée into a large bowl and let cool. Stir the shrimp into the cooled purée and coat well. Cover with plastic wrap and place in the refrigerator for 1 to 2 hours.

Place the remaining purée in a sauce pan, add the orange juice and brown sugar and cook, over medium heat, stirring occasionally, for approximately 10 minutes.

Stir the shrimp again and remove from the bowl. Discard the purée marinade. Place the shrimp on a medium-hot grill. Brush the shrimp with the orange juice and brown sugar glaze and grill for 3 to 4 minutes on each side, brushing the glaze over them two or three more times. Serve with rice and a fresh green salad.
Makes 4 Servings

3 tablespoons extra virgin olive oil
1/2 white onion, finely chopped
2 cloves garlic, minced
1 teaspoon ground cumin
1 teaspoon dried Mexican oregano
1 cup dry white wine
1/4 cup orange flavored liqueur, such as Grand Marnier or Triple Sec
1-2 chipotles in adobo sauce, chopped
1 pound (16-20 count) jumbo shrimp, peeled and deveined
1/4 cup freshly squeezed orange juice
2 tablespoons brown sugar

vegetable dishes

I often wonder why vegetables get such a bad rap. Maybe it's because many of us had overcooked, unseasoned vegetables when we were young. I think vegetables should be honored and not just served as an afterthought; therefore, this chapter is a salute to vibrant, tasty vegetables everywhere.

CHIPOTLE RICE

TO PARAPHRASE GERTRUDE STEIN'S "a rose, is a rose, is a rose," which Ernest Hemingway made fun of by saying, "an onion, is an onion, is an onion," I think rice, is rice, is rice— except when it is made with good chicken broth, sun-dried tomatoes, and chipotle.

Heat 2 tablespoons of the oil in a large saucepan. Sauté the onion for 3 to 4 minutes or until soft, but not browned. Stir in the rice and the chicken broth and simmer, covered, over low heat for 20 minutes or until the rice is tender and all the liquid has been absorbed. Stir in the sun-dried tomatoes, parsley, chipotle, salt, and pepper. Mix well.

Preheat the oven to 350° F. Coat a 2-quart Pyrex baking dish with the remaining tablespoon of oil. Spoon the rice mixture into the dish. Sprinkle the grated cheese over the top and bake for 15 minutes or until the rice is hot and the cheese has melted. This rice is a great side dish to serve with grilled fish or roasted chicken.
Makes 4 to 6 Servings

3   tablespoons extra virgin olive oil
1   large yellow onion, finely chopped
2   cups long grain rice
4   cups chicken broth
$1/4$ cup sun-dried tomatoes, chopped
1   tablespoon fresh parsley, chopped
$1 1/2$ teaspoons chipotle flakes
$1/2$ teaspoon salt
$1/4$ teaspoon ground white pepper
$1/4$ cup Romano or Parmesan cheese, grated

baked onions with an attitude

WE LOVE BAKED ONIONS, and they are so easy to prepare. They taste especially great when served with a nice, juicy steak.

Preheat oven to 375° F. or fire up your grill. Peel the onions and place them on separate squares of aluminum foil large enough to completely wrap around each onion.

In a small bowl, mix the olive oil and the melted butter together and pour over the onions. In a separate bowl, mix the garlic powder and chipotle powder together and sprinkle on top of the oil-coated onions. Wrap each onion tightly with the foil and bake for 45 minutes or until the onions are nice and soft. If you're using a grill, cook the onions for 20 minutes, turning frequently. *Makes 4 Servings*

4	large yellow onions
4	teaspoons olive oil
4	teaspoons butter, melted
1	teaspoon garlic powder
2	teaspoons chipotle powder

hoppin' john

I GREW UP IN a Yankee household where New Year's Day dinner could be anything, especially since my father was very inventive with food. I remember that he always tried to shock the more staid members of the family by serving rattlesnake canapés, Limburger cheese, and real goose liver pâté.

Then I married a southerner and quickly learned that if we didn't have ham, black-eyed peas, and cornbread for New Year's Day dinner, we'd have more bad luck than if we had broken a mirror, walked under a ladder, and let a black cat cross our path. So in honor of southern hospitality, here is a great recipe for black-eyed peas, and you don't have to wait until New Year's to try it.

Place the black-eyed peas in a bowl and add enough water to cover. Soak overnight.

The next day, drain and rinse the peas. Put them in a large saucepan or medium soup pot with 6 cups of water, the onion, bay leaf, and parsley. Bring to a boil over high heat, reduce the heat to low, and simmer, covered, for 45 minutes or until the peas are done. Remove the bay leaf and discard.

While the peas are cooking, fry the bacon for 2 to 3 minutes. Stir in the chipotle and continue to fry the bacon until crisp. When the peas are cooked, spoon the bacon and chipotle, with the drippings, into the peas. Add the rice to the pea mixture, stir, and cook over low heat, covered, for approximately 20 minutes or until the rice is done. Stir in the butter and add salt and pepper to taste. Turn the heat off and let sit for 15 minutes, covered, before serving. This black-eyed pea mixture makes a great side dish to serve with baked ham, coleslaw, and cornbread. *Makes 6 to 8 Servings*

1 cup dried black-eyed peas
6 cups water
1 medium yellow onion, chopped
1 bay leaf
1 tablespoon fresh parsley, chopped, or 1 teaspoon dried parsley
2 slices bacon, coarsely chopped
2 chipotles, stems removed and finely diced
2 cups long grain rice
2 tablespoons butter
Salt, to taste
Freshly ground black pepper, to taste

chipotle and garlic mashed potatoes

GARLIC MASHED POTATOES have been the "in" thing for some time. However, cooking the potatoes with bay leaves and then adding chipotle makes you wonder why *this* isn't the "in" thing. Refer to the photo on page 58 for a delicious serving suggestion.

Put the potatoes, kosher salt, and bay leaves in a large saucepan. Cover with water and bring to a boil over high heat. Reduce the heat to medium, cover, and cook the potatoes for 30 minutes or until tender. When the potatoes are cooked through, drain the water and discard the bay leaves. Mash the potatoes to desired consistency. Stir in the garlic, cream cheese, butter, chipotle, salt, and pepper. Whisk or beat until smooth. Serve warm with your favorite entrée.
Makes 4 to 6 Servings

5   large white potatoes, peeled and
       cut into quarters
$1/2$ teaspoon kosher salt
2   bay leaves
4   cloves garlic, roasted, peeled,
       and finely chopped
1   (4-ounce) package cream cheese,
       at room temperature
$1/4$ cup butter, at room temperature
2   teaspoons chipotle powder
$1/4$ teaspoon salt
$1/4$ teaspoon ground white pepper

farmer's market sautéed okra, corn, and tomatoes

WE ALWAYS LOOK forward to the great summer offerings at our local Farmer's Market. The corn, okra, and tomatoes all ripen about the same time, and the combination makes a terrific side dish when served with chicken breasts, pork chops or salmon.

Heat the olive oil or bacon drippings in a large cast iron skillet. Add the chopped onion and cook for 2 to 3 minutes over medium-high heat. Add the okra and the corn and cook for another 2 to 3 minutes, stirring occasionally. Add the tomato, parsley, cumin, chipotle, vinegar, sugar, and salt. Stir, turn the heat to low, cover, and let cook, stirring occasionally, for 10 minutes or until the corn and okra are done. Remove the cover and let simmer over low heat for 2 to 3 minutes more. Serve warm with your favorite chicken or pork dish.
Makes 4 Servings

4 tablespoons olive oil or bacon drippings
1 medium yellow onion, coarsely chopped
2 cups okra, sliced
2 cups corn, cut from the cob
1 medium tomato, coarsely chopped
1 teaspoon dried parsley, crushed
1/4 teaspoon ground cumin
1 teaspoon chipotle powder
1 tablespoon distilled white vinegar
1 teaspoon sugar
1/2 teaspoon salt

OPPOSITE: *Salmon Steaks with Chipotle Mustard (recipe on page 62) and Farmer's Market Sautéed Okra, Corn, and Tomatoes (recipe above).*

CORN ON THE COB WITH BLUE RIBBON CHIPOTLE BUTTER

NOTHING BEATS CORN on the cob for great summertime eating, and it is especially good when accompanied by my blue ribbon chipotle butter. You can also use this spicy butter to flavor popcorn. Just pop the corn and drizzle the chipotle butter over the top.

To boil the corn, start by husking the corn and removing all of the silk. Place the corn in a large pot, cover with water, add the salt and the milk, and bring to a boil. Reduce the heat and simmer until the corn is tender, approximately 10 minutes.

Meanwhile, put the butter in a microwave safe bowl and microwave on high for 2 minutes or until the butter has melted. Stir in the chipotle powder, lime juice, and salt and microwave on high for 30 seconds more. Mix well. Using a pastry brush, generously brush the corn with the chipotle butter. Serve immediately. *Makes 4 to 6 Servings*

CORN:
4-8 ears fresh yellow corn
1 teaspoon kosher salt
1 cup milk

BUTTER:
$\frac{1}{2}$ pound butter
1-2 teaspoons chipotle powder
Juice of 1 lime
Pinch kosher salt

cheese and asparagus strata

OUR SMALL SOUTHERN NEW MEXICO town has a street fair every Labor Day, and we always have a house full of guests who spend long, tiring, hot days selling homemade jewelry, watches, jams, and stuffed toys to the burgeoning crowds. Since there is very little time to eat lunch, we prepare a strata ahead of time. All we have to do is pop it in the oven and serve.

Cut the large, tough ends of the asparagus off, and then lay the asparagus in a large non-stick skillet. Cover with water and cook over medium heat until tender, but still crisp. Drain and let cool.

Spray a 13 x 9-inch glass Pyrex baking dish with vegetable cooking spray. Brush one side of 6 slices of the bread with the melted butter and place the slices in the baking dish, butter side down. Wrap each cooled asparagus spear with a slice of prosciutto or ham and place on top of the bread.

Mix the Cheddar and Parmesan together and sprinkle half of the mixture on the asparagus and prosciutto. Cover and reserve the other half of the cheese mixture. Brush the remaining 6 slices of bread with the rest of the butter and lay the slices of bread, buttered side up, on top of the prosciutto wrapped asparagus and cheese.

In a separate bowl, lightly beat the eggs with a whisk, and then whisk in the milk. Stir in the onion flakes and the chipotle powder and pour over the bread. Cover with plastic wrap and refrigerate overnight.

About an hour before serving, preheat the oven to 325° F. Take the strata out of the refrigerator and remove the plastic wrap. Bake for 45 minutes, remove from the oven, and sprinkle the remaining cheese on top. Return the dish to the oven and bake for another 15 minutes or until the cheese is hot and bubbly. Serve hot or at room temperature. *Makes 6 to 8 Servings*

12 thin asparagus spears
1 (1-pound) loaf Texas Toast (approximately 12 thick slices white bread)
4 tablespoons butter, melted
12 thin slices prosciutto or ham
1 cup Cheddar cheese, shredded
½ cup Parmesan cheese, grated
6 large eggs
3 cups milk
1 tablespoon dehydrated onion flakes
2 teaspoons chipotle powder

individual cheese and chipotle soufflés

IN THE SEVENTIES, my wife and I opened a French restaurant in southern New Mexico. The star attraction was our amazing individual soufflé that took only minutes to get to the table. So, the next time you want to impress your guests, astound them with this unique offering. They will think you spent all day preparing these delicious soufflés.

Preheat the oven to 375° F. Melt the butter in the top of a double boiler directly on the burner over medium heat. Whisk in the flour, and then stir in the milk. Add the chipotle powder and salt and take the pan off the heat. Let cool slightly, and then, one at a time, vigorously beat in the egg yolks. (Be sure to let cool slightly and to beat vigorously or else you'll have egg drop soup). Set aside.

Put hot water in the bottom of the double boiler and place the top of the double boiler over the water. Stir in the cheese until it is completely melted. Remove the top of the double boiler from the hot water and let the mixture cool slightly again.

In a separate bowl, beat the egg whites until they are just becoming stiff, and then add a pinch of cream of tartar. Beat again until the mixture is stiff. Fold the egg whites into the egg yolk mixture in the top of the double boiler.

Spoon the mixture into 4 (1-cup) generously buttered soufflé dishes or deep ramekins. Bake in the preheated oven for approximately 12 to 15 minutes, or until the tops are a delicate golden brown. Carefully remove the soufflé dishes, place them on small serving plates, put a sprig of cilantro on the plate, and serve immediately. *Makes 4 Servings*

2 tablespoons butter
2 tablespoons all-purpose flour
$\frac{3}{4}$ cup whole milk
$\frac{1}{2}$ teaspoon chipotle powder
$\frac{1}{4}$ teaspoon salt
4 egg yolks
1 cup Gruyere cheese, grated
5 egg whites
Pinch cream of tartar
4 sprigs cilantro

CHILE RELLENOS ARE ONE OF MY FAVORITE New Mexican dishes. However, deep fat frying them is such a hassle that I have started baking them. And, baking the chiles in a casserole dish means that we can still have the rich, satisfying taste of fresh green chiles without having to clean the deep fat fryer. In this recipe, the chipotle gives an added zing that is just right for a great brunch offering, especially when it is served with a fresh melon compote.

Preheat oven to 350° F. Coat the bottom and sides of glass baking dish or an ovenproof ceramic casserole dish with the oil. Place the chiles, side by side, in the bottom of the dish. Sprinkle the cheese over the chiles.

Place the eggs in a food processor and pulse. Add the milk, flour, salt, pepper, cumin, oregano, and chipotle and blend until smooth. Pour the egg mixture over the cheese and chiles and bake for 30 minutes or until the mixture has set and is lightly browned. Cut the casserole into equal portions, trying to give each person one whole green chile. *Makes 4 to 6 Servings*

1 tablespoon extra virgin olive oil

8-10 large, whole New Mexico, Anaheim, or Poblano green chiles, roasted, peeled, stems removed, and seeded

1 pound Cheddar cheese, grated

3 large eggs

2 cups milk

$\frac{1}{2}$ cup all-purpose flour

1 teaspoon salt

$\frac{1}{2}$ teaspoon freshly ground black pepper

$\frac{1}{2}$ teaspoon ground cumin

$\frac{1}{2}$ teaspoon ground oregano

4 chipotles in adobo sauce, chopped

easy CORN bake

THIS IS ONE OF THOSE SIMPLE, easy-to-make delicious dishes that when one of the neighbors brings it to a potluck, you get mad at yourself. Why didn't you think of it, you wonder, instead of the frozen broccoli topped with Cheddar cheese you heated in the microwave as you walked out the door. This dish also makes a great side for Thanksgiving dinner!

Preheat oven to 325° F. Melt the butter in a skillet. Sauté the onion and bell pepper for 2 to 3 minutes over low heat. Add the green chiles and corn and cook for 4 to 5 minutes more. Spray a 2-quart glass baking dish with vegetable spray. Spoon the onion and corn mixture into the dish.

Put the eggs, chipotle, and salt in a blender. Blend until the eggs are lightly beaten. Add the milk and half-and-half and blend. Add the flour and blend until smooth.

Pour the egg mixture over the vegetables and put the baking dish into a pan of hot water, making sure that the water does not come more than half way up the sides of the dish (the water bath will prevent the casserole from burning on the bottom). Place the water bath and the baking dish in the oven and bake for 45 minutes or until the egg mixture is set and lightly browned. Remove the dish from the oven and the water bath. Sprinkle the cheese over top and let sit for 3 to 4 minutes until the cheese melts. Serve immediately.
Makes 4 to 6 Servings

2 tablespoons butter
½ medium yellow onion, chopped
1 medium red bell pepper, seeded and chopped
2 Anaheim or New Mexico green chiles, roasted, peeled, seeded, and chopped, or 1 (4-ounce) can chopped green chiles
2 cups corn, cut off the cob, or 2 cups frozen corn
4 eggs
1 teaspoon chipotle powder
½ teaspoon salt
1 cup milk
1 cup half-and-half
⅓ cup all-purpose flour
½ cup Cheddar cheese, grated

fiery vegetarian Lasagna

I AM AN UNABASHED MEAT EATER. However, to paraphrase Will Rogers, I also never met a vegetable I didn't like. So needless to say, several vegetarian dishes have found their way into my repertoire over the years. This richly flavored, layered combination of tomatoes, zucchini, spinach, and olives laced with the fire of chipotle will win over even the most ardent steak-and-potatoes lover.

Preheat oven to 350° F. Cook the lasagna noodles according to the package directions. While the pasta is cooking, heat the oil in a skillet and sauté the onion and garlic until they start to soften. Stir in the parsley, cilantro, salt, pepper, basil, and oregano. Add the tomatoes and the chipotle and simmer for 4 to 5 minutes. Set aside.

In a medium bowl, beat the eggs for approximately 1 minute, and then slowly beat the ricotta cheese into the eggs a little at a time.

Drain the cooked lasagna noodles and lay one half of them in the bottom of a lightly greased 9 x 13-inch baking pan. Make sure the noodles overlap. Spread half of the ricotta mixture on the noodles, and then layer half of the cooked spinach, zucchini, olives, mozzarella, and Cheddar cheese on top of the ricotta mixture. Top with half of the cooked tomato and chipotle mixture. Repeat the process, sprinkle the Romano or Parmesan cheese on the very top, and bake for 45 minutes or until heated through and bubbly. Serve with a tossed green salad, bruschetta, and a glass of dry red wine. *Makes 4 to 6 Servings*

1 (10-ounce) package lasagna noodles
2 tablespoons extra virgin olive oil
1 medium yellow onion, finely chopped
2 cloves garlic, finely minced
2 tablespoons fresh parsley, chopped
1 tablespoon fresh cilantro, finely chopped
1 teaspoon salt
1/2 teaspoon freshly ground black pepper
1/2 teaspoon dried basil
1 teaspoon dried Mexican oregano, crushed
3 1/2 cups ripe tomatoes, peeled and diced
1 (7-ounce) can chipotles in adobo sauce, puréed
2 eggs
1 pound ricotta cheese
2 cups spinach, cooked, diced, and well-drained
1 cup zucchini, scrubbed and diced
1/2 cup black olives, sliced
1 cup mozzarella cheese, grated
1 cup Cheddar cheese, grated
1/2 cup Romano or Parmesan cheese, freshly grated

special touches

Okay, so you got the basics down, and now you need that little something extra that takes ordinary food to a new level. Whether you rub it on, shake it on, or dip it, any dish is extra special with one of these *special touches*.

CANTALOUPE SALSA

MANGO SALSA

CINCO DE MAYO SALSA

AVOCADO AND JICAMA SALSA

FIREWORKS SALSA

CHIPOTLE BARBECUE SAUCE

CHIPOTLE RUB

SOUTHWESTERN MARINADE

CHIPOTLE RED SAUCE

CHIPOTLE BUTTER

CHIPOTLE MAYONNAISE

cantaLoupe saLsa

SEVERAL YEARS AGO we spent a couple of months house-sitting a lovely casita in West Hollywood. One afternoon we were shopping in a local supermarket and drew a small crowd. I was pushing in the stem ends of the cantaloupes and sniffing them to see which was the ripest. Even in the casual ambiance of southern California, people were fascinated by my unscientific process of selecting the best melon. But believe me—it works!

Put all of the ingredients in a medium bowl and lightly mix. Refrigerate for 1 hour so that the flavors can blend. Serve with tortilla chips.
Makes approximately 3 cups

1 medium cantaloupe, peeled, seeded, and diced
$\frac{1}{2}$ medium red onion, diced
1 green bell pepper, seeded and diced
2 chipotles in adobo sauce, rinsed and finely diced
1 tablespoon fresh cilantro, finely chopped
$\frac{1}{4}$ teaspoon ground cinnamon
1 teaspoon salt
1 teaspoon freshly ground black pepper
3 tablespoons lime juice
2 tablespoons orange juice
1 tablespoon gold tequila

maNgo saLsa

THESE DAYS, mangos are readily available in most supermarkets, and they are extremely versatile. One of our favorite ways to use mangos is in this salsa, which is very tasty and extremely refreshing on a warm summer day. Spoon this salsa over grilled tuna, sliced pork roast, or tortilla chips.

Mix all of the ingredients together and refrigerate for up to 1 hour before serving in order to let the flavors blend.

Makes approximately 2 cups

- 1 medium mango, peeled, seeded, and coarsely chopped
- $1/2$ red onion, diced
- 2 chipotles in adobo sauce, rinsed and chopped
- 1 tablespoon fresh cilantro, chopped
- $1/4$ teaspoon salt
- $1/4$ teaspoon ground white pepper
- $1/4$ cup fresh lime juice

cinco de mayo salsa

EVERYONE IN THE SOUTHWEST uses Cinco de Mayo as an excuse to party, and what better way to celebrate than with a nice, fresh bowl of colorful salsa. If you are serving this tasty salsa to wimps, reduce the amount of chipotle. However, if your guests are natural fire breathers, you can experiment by adding even more chipotle.

Mix all of the ingredients together in a bowl. Place in the refrigerator for 1 hour before serving. This salsa is not only great with chips, but it is also the perfect accompaniment to grilled chicken and hamburgers.

Makes approximately 3 cups

1	red bell pepper, seeded and chopped
1	green bell pepper, seeded and chopped
2	cups fresh pineapple, cubed, or 1 (20-ounce) can pineapple chunks, drained
2	teaspoons chipotle powder
1/2	medium red onion, diced
1	tablespoon fresh lime juice
2	tablespoons fresh cilantro, chopped

avocado and jicama salsa

WE OFTEN SERVE bowls of guacamole, sliced jicama, sliced onion, and salsa on a buffet. One day, we were in too much of a hurry to make individual bowls of everything, so we just mixed it all together and came up with this ying-yang salsa. It pleases the palate with its combination of velvety smooth avocado and crunchy jicama.

Place the avocado chunks in a medium-sized bowl. Stir in the lime juice so that the avocado is well coated. Gently stir in the remaining ingredients. Serve with tortilla chips or over grilled fish. *Makes approximately 4 cups*

2 large, firm, ripe Haas avocados, peeled, pitted, and diced
$^1/_3$ cup fresh lime juice
1 medium jicama, peeled and diced
$^1/_2$ medium red onion, finely diced
1 clove garlic, minced
2 chipotles, finely chopped
$^1/_4$ cup fresh cilantro, coarsely chopped
$^1/_2$ teaspoon salt

fireworks salsa

THIS SALSA IS A DELIGHTFUL FUSION of the Far East and the Southwest, as it combines the rich flavors of chipotle and ginger. This salsa will truly make any special occasion party come alive.

Place the avocados, chipotle, lemon juice, ginger, and salt in a food processor and pulse until well blended but not smooth. Spoon into a serving bowl and sprinkle the green onions over the top. Place the bowl on a platter, and surround it with your favorite chips. This salsa is also great when served over grilled fish or chicken.

Makes approximately 2 cups

2 avocados, peeled, seeded, and quartered
1 teaspoon chipotle powder
1 tablespoon lemon juice
1 tablespoon sweet, pickled ginger, diced, or 1 tablespoon fresh ginger, grated
$\frac{1}{2}$ teaspoon salt
2 green onions with the white portion and some of the green portion, sliced

chipotle barbecue sauce

THERE ARE A LOT OF GOOD bottled barbecue sauces on the market. However, when we want the perfect blend of chipotle, spices, brown sugar, and marmalade, we make our own sauce.

Heat the oil in a heavy deep skillet or saucepan and sauté the onion for 2 to 3 minutes. Add the garlic and sauté for 2 to 3 more minutes or until the onion is soft. Add the rest of the ingredients and simmer over low heat until the flavors have combined, approximately 30 minutes. Store in the refrigerator until ready to use with any of your favorite entrées. This sauce will keep for up to a week in the refrigerator. *Makes approximately 5 cups*

- 2 tablespoons extra virgin olive oil
- 1 large yellow onion, chopped
- 2 cloves garlic, minced
- 1 teaspoon dry yellow mustard
- 3 cups tomato sauce
- 1 cup red wine
- 1 cup water
- 1/4 cup lemon juice
- 1 cup Worcestershire sauce
- 1/2 cup brown sugar
- 1/2 cup orange marmalade
- 1 teaspoon salt
- 1 (7-ounce) can chipotle in adobo sauce, puréed

chipotle rub

I USED TO DO RUBS long before I knew what they were called. Like so many food terms, the nomenclature often catches up to me long after I've done it. This particular rub is great for steaks, chicken, and pork chops. We particularly like to use it on rib-eye steaks.

Mix all of the ingredients together in a large, shallow bowl. Place your chosen meat in the bowl, one piece at a time, and rub the spice mixture all over each piece of meat. When each piece is well coated, sauté, bake, or grill your entrée to desired doneness. *Makes approximately 1/2 cup*

- 1 tablespoon chipotle powder
- 1 tablespoon granulated garlic
- 1 tablespoon kosher salt
- 1 teaspoon ground cumin
- 1 teaspoon dried Mexican oregano, crushed

southwestern marinade

ALTHOUGH "SOUTHWESTERN" MEANS different things to different people, I think the combination of chipotle, chile powder, cumin, and beer is the essence of southwestern flavor.

Mix all of the ingredients together. Place the chicken, steak, or roast in a large shallow glass bowl and pour the marinade over the meat. Cover and let the meat sit in the refrigerator for 15 minutes to 1 hour. Remove the meat and discard the marinade.

Grill, broil, or roast the meat as you normally would and enjoy the wonderful smoky flavor of the chipotle marinade.

Makes approximately 2 cups

1 (12-ounce) can beer
1/4 cup TABASCO® brand Chipotle Pepper Sauce
1 tablespoon New Mexico red chile powder
2 tablespoons Worcestershire sauce
1 tablespoon extra virgin olive oil
1 teaspoon dry mustard
1/2 teaspoon ground cumin
2 cloves garlic, run through a garlic press

chipotle red sauce

MOST SOUTHWESTERN COOKS make a traditional red chile sauce with dried red New Mexico chiles. This recipe adds the smoothness of tomato sauce and the smoky flavor of chipotle, resulting in a wonderfully lush sauce that is hard to beat. Serve this sauce on the side with Happy Holiday Posole (page 43) or with any dish that calls for a deep, fiery, rich red sauce.

Heat 1 tablespoon of the olive oil in a medium saucepan and sauté the onion and garlic until soft. Remove the onions and garlic to a plate and heat the remaining 2 tablespoons of oil in the pan. Whisk in the flour and lightly brown but do not let burn. Add the chicken broth and whisk until smooth. Add the tomato sauce and the chipotle. Stir back in the onions and garlic, and simmer over very low heat, stirring occasionally, until smooth and well blended. Add more chicken broth or water if necessary to adjust the thickness of the sauce.

Makes approximately 2 cups

3 tablespoons extra virgin olive oil
1/2 medium yellow onion, chopped
2 cloves garlic, minced
2 tablespoons all-purpose flour
1 (14-ounce) can chicken broth
1 cup tomato sauce
1 (7-ounce) can chipotle in adobo sauce, finely diced

chipotle butter

TRY BRUSHING A LITTLE of this spicy butter over a grilled steak just before serving it to your friends or family. Stand back and listen to their rave reviews!

Put all of the ingredients in a food processor and pulse until well blended and smooth. Spoon the processed butter into a bowl, cover with plastic wrap, and keep in the refrigerator until ready to use. Put a spoonful on top of a grilled steak just before serving or spread the chipotle butter on sliced French bread and serve as a side with a luncheon salad. *Makes approximately 1 cup*

- 1/2 pound (2 sticks) unsalted butter, cut into tablespoons
- 2 green onions, with some of the green part, finely chopped
- 1/4 cup dry white wine
- 1 teaspoon chipotle powder

chipotle mayonnaise

ONE OF THE THINGS I LEARNED when attending cooking classes in the sixties was how to make mayonnaise from scratch. We were told that you were not a "real chef" unless you could master it. Those times are long gone, and I rarely make my own anymore. Now I prefer to take a good commercial mayonnaise and add all sorts of things to it to make it special for use with salads and sandwiches. This chipotle mayonnaise vies with Russian dressing as one of our favorites when spread on steak, chicken, or corned beef sandwiches.

Combine all of the ingredients and mix well. Refrigerate for approximately 1 hour before serving so that the flavors can blend. *Makes approximately 1 1/4 cups*

- 1 cup good commercial mayonnaise
- 1 teaspoon ground cumin
- 1/4 cup ketchup
- Juice of one lime
- 1 teaspoon chipotle powder

resources

The following list offers just a few of the many sites you will find by searching the Internet using the word chipotle. Each site provides a wealth of information about products that contain chipotle, but as these sites change from time to time, remember to keep searching until you find the quantity, price, and product that is just right for you. And the most important part? Have fun experimenting!

CHILE TODAY–HOT TAMALE
(800) Hot-Pepper
www.chiletoday.com
Dried chipotle and chipotle powder sold online by
Rol and David, "The Heat Brothers."

FRENCH'S
(800) 442-4733
http://frenchsmustard.com/
French's Chipotle Chili Mayonnaise is available
online and in supermarkets.

THE GENERAL STORE (A Division of Alan's Kitchen)
(602) 320-2771
www.alanskitchen.com
Chipotle barbecue rubs, sauces, dip mixes, and salsas
available online.

GOURMET SLEUTH
(408) 354-8281
www.gourmetsleuth.com
Canned chipotle in adobo, dried chipotle ahumado
peppers, and chipotle powder available online.

THE GREAT AMERICAN SPICE COMPANY
(888) 502-8058
www.americanspice.com
Buffalo Chipotle Mexican Hot Sauce available online.

MCCORMICK
(800) 632-5847
www.mccormick.com
Chipotle Chile Pepper, Mesquite Grilling Sauce,
Mesquite Marinade, and their newest spice blend,
Rattlesnake Shake, available online or in grocery stores.

MCILHENNY COMPANY
(800) 634-9599
www.TABASCO.com
TABASCO® brand Chipotle Pepper Sauce
available online and in supermarkets.

CIBOLO JUNCTION FOOD AND SPICE COMPANY
(505) 689-1034
Ground chipotle and chipotle pods are just some of
the many chiles offered by this company.

CHEF PAUL PRUDHOMME'S
MAGIC SEASONING BLENDS
(800) 457-2857
www.chefpaul.com
Specialties include Southwest Chipotle Marinade and
Ground, Dried Magic Chile.

OLDE WESTPORT SPICE & TRADING COMPANY
(800) 537-6470
www.oldewestportspice.com
Featuring the Prairie Fire Chipotle Pepper Blend,
which is available online.

PEPPER FOOL
(323) 578-5603
www.pepperfool.com
Chipotles available by the ounce or the pound.

SAM MCGEES
(208) 762-3367
www.SamMcGees.com
A wide range of chipotle sauces, including Not Cool
Hickory Smoked Chipotle Sauce.

index

index

index

Index compiled by Jan Williams,
Indexing Services

LYNN NUSOM comes from a strong family tradition of working in the food industry, so it was natural that he follow in the same footsteps. Throughout his career, he owned and operated several restaurants, and he was the executive chef at a four-star, four-diamond hotel. He is currently a successful restaurant consultant.

Lynn is the author of ten cookbooks and has written a weekly food column for the past twenty years. While traveling to conduct cooking seminars and to promote his books, he continues to expand his culinary repertoire. Lynn lives with his wife, Guylyn Morris Nusom, in a restored historic adobe home in southern New Mexico.